Forensic Sculpting
Step-by-step
In Photos

Seth Wolfson
©Realsculpt Press 2005

Dedication and thanks,

This book is dedicated to all of the people who have helped me in my life and work - My friends, family and especially Lorna, my old ball and chain, for supporting my efforts and following me around the country, kicking my butt in gear, and most of all putting up with me. I would like to thank Thea at FX Warehouse, Amy Wieck for being my lifecasting and figure-making partner, Bensalem PD and Danny Sollitti for helping me with my first real case, Todd Mathews and The Doe Network,Billy bob, Rich and the fig fin gang for teaching me about skins and scenic art. Finally Mike Defeo for teaching me all the skills to be an fx artist and sculptor,I never would have been a professional artist without his help.

I want to give a special thanks to Jen Pullinger for editing my book, It would have been a one long, misspelled, run-on sentence with out her help and skill!

PREFACE

Having practiced forensic sculpting for many years and learning by apprenticeship in fields that had very few books and no schools at the time, I have noticed that most books about make-up fx sculpting frequently lack much of the actual sculpting "how-to" instruction. Even sculpting textbooks leave out incredibly easy methods that can produce hyper-realistic detail. With "Forensic Sculpting: Step-by-Step In Photos," I am going to impart the methods typically kept from the novice and only picked up through years of work experience. These methods are not usually taught in schools or even notable art colleges, but are what the best artists use to create their famous works in bronze and marble, film and medical prosthetics, and even wax figures.

I will also concentrate on the practical and measurement-based beginnings to these methods and explain some tips, tricks, and the do's and don'ts. Safety will be stressed. Forensic sculpting can be a career, but in the beginning a signficant amount of practice is required. It can be a slighty unsafe avocation if not approached with care. I suggest following the book step-by-step, including the use of materials so that you know what your final result should look like. Keep in mind there are always variations. It should look like a sketch of my version as seen in the photos; it does not have to be an exact rendering of my example.

Afterwards, I recommend buying a forensic sculpting model skull, in particular one that is accompanied by a photo of the person. These skulls will be used to test your skill. The model skulls come with a sealed envelope containing the photo. After you complete the techniques I have demonstrated, open the envelope and see if it's correct! I recommend letting someone else check your work. This way, if you need to redo it, you still won't know what the person's features look like and can then continue developing your skills on the same skull without going through the expense of purchasing a new one. Attempt taking the test again with your model skull.

Never stop taking sculpting lessons. I recommend taking at least one sculpting class a year, or at least be willing to learn from the people around you. Even the novice sculptor can teach the expert something. I also recommend taking one of the great forensic sculpting workshops available. Eventually you will find your confidence.

There are tools referenced in this book that are not for use by unsupervised children. Make sure that an adult helps with drilling, gluing, and knife use.

This book is for the training of forensic sculpters only; you must refer to your local, state, national, and international guidelines for "chain of evidence" rules on how to handle a real skull. You should also insist that the real skull be pre-cleaned before it arrives. Real skulls are extremely fragile. You are responsible for any damage.

Always refer to an anthropologist for information on the skulls age, race, sex, ect. You can guess for practice purposes, but on a real case refer to the professionals.

Make sure to properly research your duties, responsibilities, and have all required paperwork before accepting a case.

On this project we will pretend that this skull is a male and use the "normal" chart. This will allow for larger features to aid in learning how to sculpt in clay for the novice. As stated above I would need an anthropologist to determine the proper information about the skull such as sex, age, and race.

WORK SMART AND WORK SAFE.

CONTENTS

PART ONE: MATERIALS

Materials should cost less than $100. Most are reusable. Many of these items can be purchased from your local hardware or art supply store and through make-up supply stores listed in the phonebook or on the internet. Don't be thrifty; get the best sculpting tools you can afford. The better the tools, the easier it will be to learn how to sculpt the proper way. Cheap plastiline or water clays will not work well or at all. There is only one flesh-tone plastiline readily available at most art stores; it comes in economy sizes.

www.fxwarehouseinc.com
Sculpting tools (pro set) or one with a "thin line" tool
Red & sm.black stipple sponge
28mm Glass or plastic eyes balls
10 bricks of **flesh** colored sulfur free clay

www.alconeco.com
Wig - if needed

www.anatomical.com
"Budget two-piece skull"

Market/deptartment store
Plastic wrap
Cotton balls
Newspaper
Rubbing alcohol
Rolling board
Long vinyl erasers
Rolling pin
digital camera with a macro feature (denoted by a flower icon)

Hardware or art supply
1 12x12 ¼" thick piece of plywood
1 pipe flange 1/4"
1 12" pipe that is threaded to fit the pipe flage
Masking tape
Glue Cynoacrylate type
Hobby knife / utility knife
Safety glasses
Mm ruler
Mm calipers
Stencil brushs
Indelible marker
Plastic skull
Wood screws
Drill

PART TWO: CLAYS

REFRIGERATE THE CLAY FOR THIS PROJECT FOR AT LEAST 2 HOURS.

This will ensure that it's firm. Even though most people think soft clay is better because it's easier to work between their fingers, it's absolutely the worst way to mold! The flesh-colored plastiline is very soft, and will not cut properly into the needed strips, which can easily cause you to mess up your sculpture. When using clay to create realistic objects such as people, you will need to sculpt fine details. In the case of a human head form, soft clay can easily dent and details will not "carve in."

The first type is sulfur free plastiline. That is what we are using. There are many brands and many colors from which to choose. I recommend using the flesh tone for this project, but *only* for this type of work. This color will look good in a black and white photo. You can use alcohol or water to smooth it out. Water does not evaporate, however so I recommend the alcohol. These clays also will not affect silicones.

When buying clay, there are different types from which to choose. The first is water clay or pottery clay. This is used for kiln-baked sculptures, large sculptures, and art class sculptures. This clay is cheap so many sculptors use it. Unfortunately, it's not useful for most real world purposes. It cracks and must be kept wet. One particular brand available through www.fxwarehouseinc.com called W.E.D. clay is good for sculpting things that are large and don't need to be baked. The brand is unique; it's the best water clay for sculpting items you want to mold, not bake. The main solvent that smoothes it is water.

The second type of clay is plastiline. This is an oil-based clay that usually contains sulfur. It's the best for sculpting faces, but it only comes in gray or white, which is why I don't use it for this application. Due to its sulfur content, it can burn your eyes if you rub them while working with it. This material will also not allow some silicones to cure against it. Keep that in mind if you are ever molding a project. This type of clay is also numbered. It's in Italian, so look for the word "libre." #1 is the softest through #4, which is the hardest. I recommend #3, or #2 if need be. You can microwave this particular clay to soften it, but be careful because the center will liquify and burn your skin easily. Plastiline clay is used in sculpting movie prosthetics. The solvents that smooth it are isopropyl alcohol, acetone, and "244 fluid" from www.alconeco.com .

Next, there is oven baked clay. It's usually in the craft section of most stores and is used for making beads or small figures. Clay that bakes into a rubbery substance is also available in that brand!

There are epoxy based clays that self-harden and become hard as a rock, great for household repairs, props, figures, repairing plaster molds or car radiators, and other fun stuff. You can use a version from your local plumbing supply store. It comes in a plastic tube. It's two clays rolled into one and a cold weld-type material. Different versions are available from auto parts places in the repair section. Ask for the two-part clays, which come in a tube or in two separate flat bars.There is a version at FX Warehouse that comes in large inexpensive sizes - much more bang for your buck than the other types. This brand is also non-toxic.

Finally, there are wax and wax/clay mixtures. These are good for jewelry sculpting, action figures, and other fine work.

Remember the solvents. When used with stencil brushes from an art supply store, they can help smooth clay. This is one trick you won't find in books of a similar subject matter, but is used in the professional sculpting field. We will discuss this further in the sculpting portions of the book.

PART THREE: SET UP

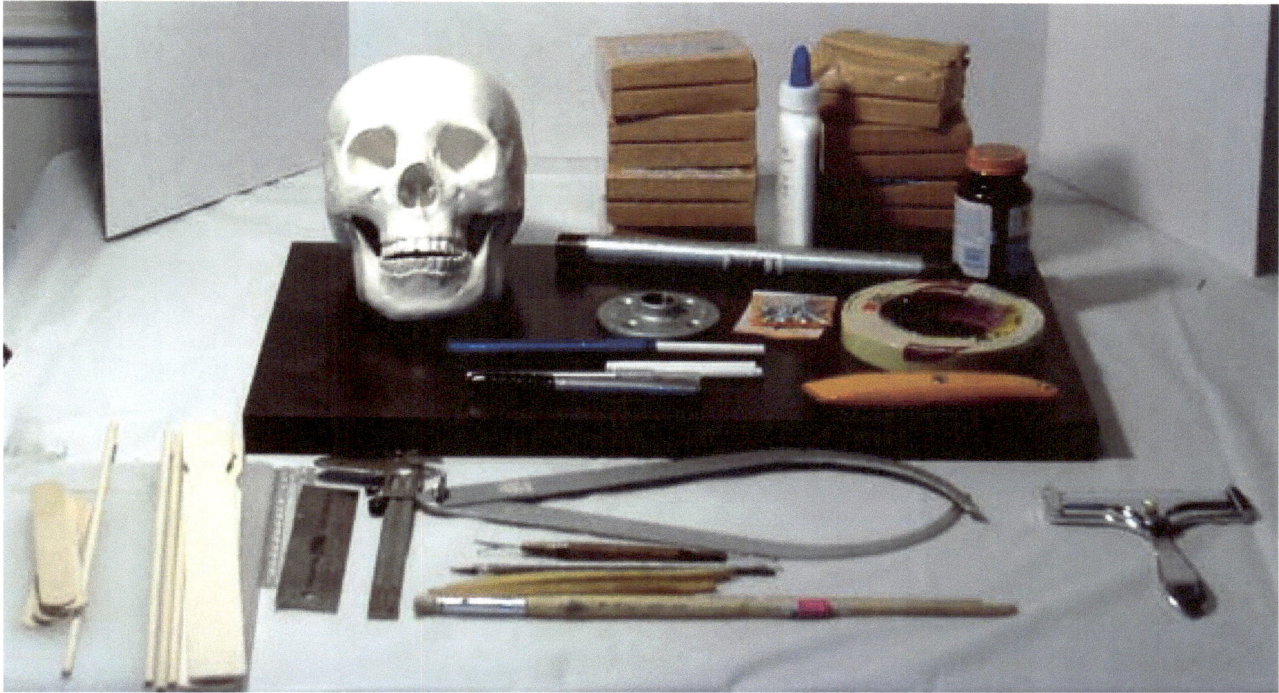

As you can see the mm. ruler, gauge, calipers and sculpting tools. Don't be afraid to ask for help at the store. Make sure you have plenty of light, and no one to disturb you while you work. If you are working on a real case, it should be done in a room that only you have access. Again, follow local and state protocol.

Tip: Make sure to cover rugs with plastic because clay will not come out of carpet.

PART FOUR: SKULL MOUNT

TOOLS AND MATERIALS NEEDED:
Drill, pipe flange, pipe, screws, and matching bit for the drill.
Remember, the tools are not for unsupervised children. Get an adult to help.

<u>WEAR SAFTEY GOOGLES WHEN USING THE DRILL!</u> When pre-drilling, to avoid splitting wood or installing screws, never apply too much pressure to the drill or put your weight on it. Doing this could potentially cause the drill bit or screw bit to "skip" and drill into your other hand. The goggles are to protect from flying debris. Note that you should never wear rubber gloves or loose clothing when using a drill. If you have long hair, tie it back. It's extremely easy to have those items catch and twist on the drill. It can rip the hair out of your head! Please be careful.

Step 1
Pre-drill holes and use a screw gun to insert the screws to secure the pipe flange. Remember your safety guidelines. Wear goggles and don't apply to too much pressure on the drill. Work safe.

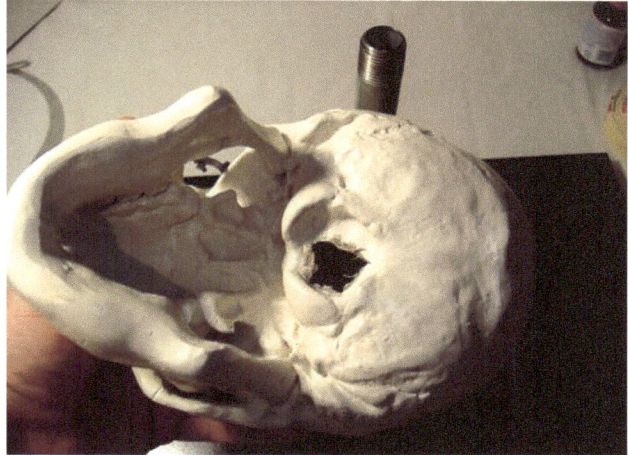

Step 3
Use the utility knife to open up a hole at the base of the skull (Foramen magnum).When using knives, always cut away from your body. Make sure that your fingers are not in the way in case you slip.

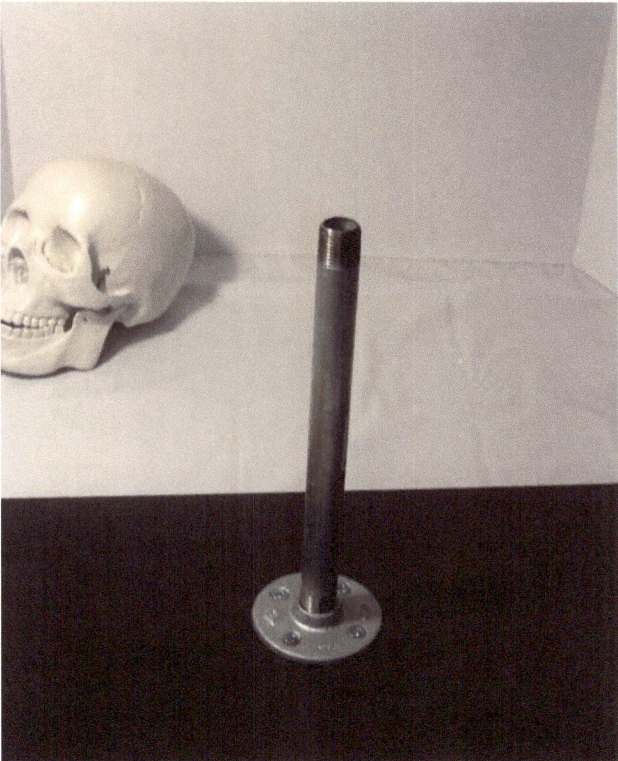

Step 2
Install the pipe into the flange.

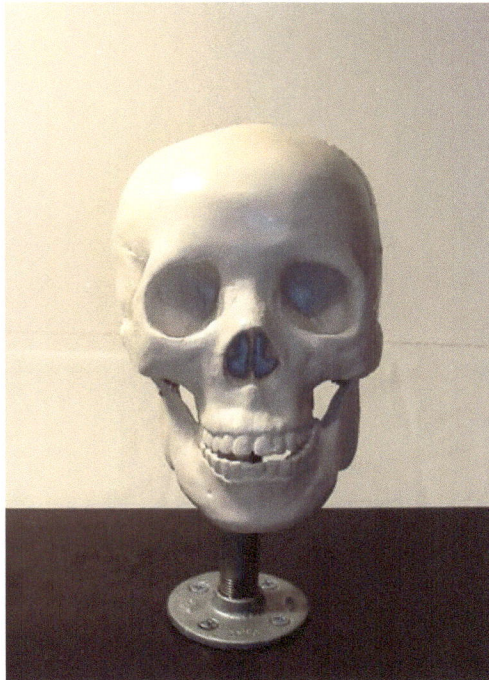

Step 4
Mount skull on pipe.(warning) With a real skull use small pipe and pad it, or just use clay. Be careful with real skulls because they are very fragile.

PART FIVE: MARKERS

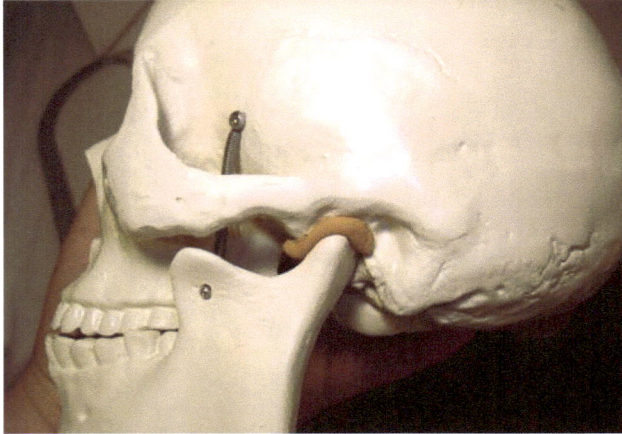

Step 5
Use clay as a spacer between the jaw bone and skull to simulate the cartilage.

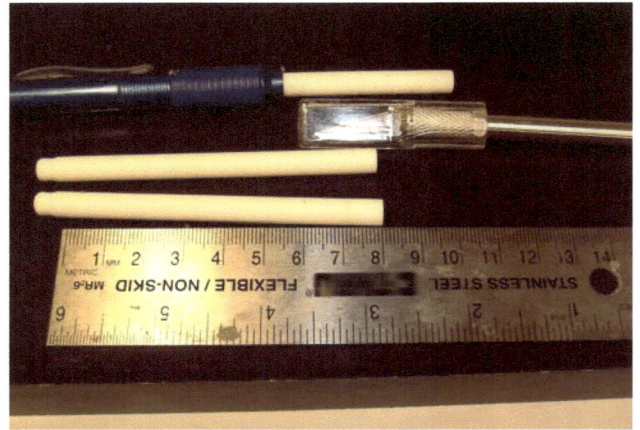

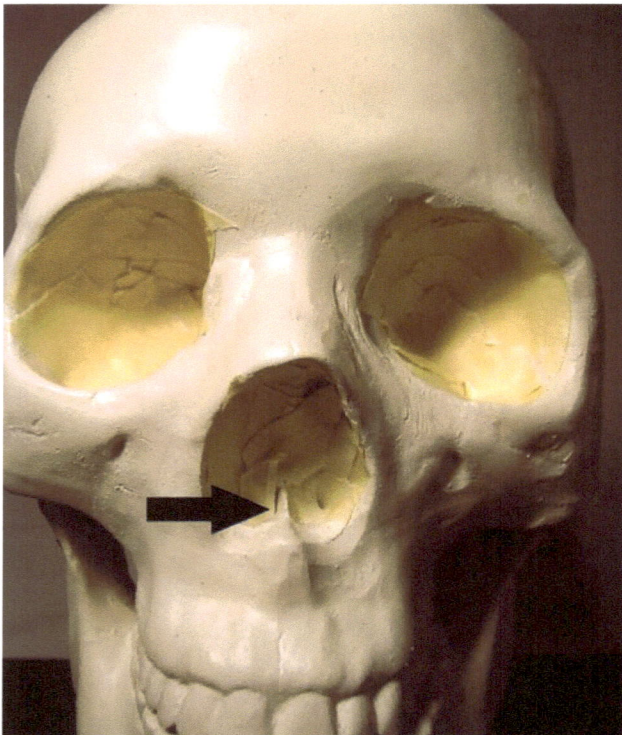

Step 6
Put cotton into the eye sockets and nasal area to protect fragile bones, and then cover carefully with masking tape. Make sure to leave the front edge of the nasal spine uncovered (the area noted by the arrow).The tape makes cleanup easy.

Step 7
Time to cut the markers. You will need a utility/hobby knife, MM ruler, gauge, and your eraser materials. Be careful not to cut your self. Please cut away from your body. **READ THE INSTRUCTIONS BEFORE CUTTING.** "Measure twice cut once."

Cut as close as possible to the measurements in the charts on the following pages, but don't feel like you need a micrometer to do it. If you are off .0002 of a millimeter, it is perfectly fine. Now, use the "normal" scale in the European male chart. I have also provided the European female and African-Negroid male and female charts for reference. I did leave out certain markers that are not used in the 3-D method. Take your time. It's to be expected that you will mess up frequently the first few times you do this. Make sure you **cut two of each marker.** You won't actually need two, but it's better to have an extra for backup. You can find the eraser material in the office supply section of many stores. I recommend getting six erasers so you have enough. Buy a good indelible marker, keeping in mind it will not come out of clothes and is hard to wash off from skin (it usually wears off in a day or so). Try to cut straight, or markers may fall to the wrong angle under the clay. On the nose and thin spots, that can be a problem. Here is how to cut properly measured markers with little deviance from the chart.

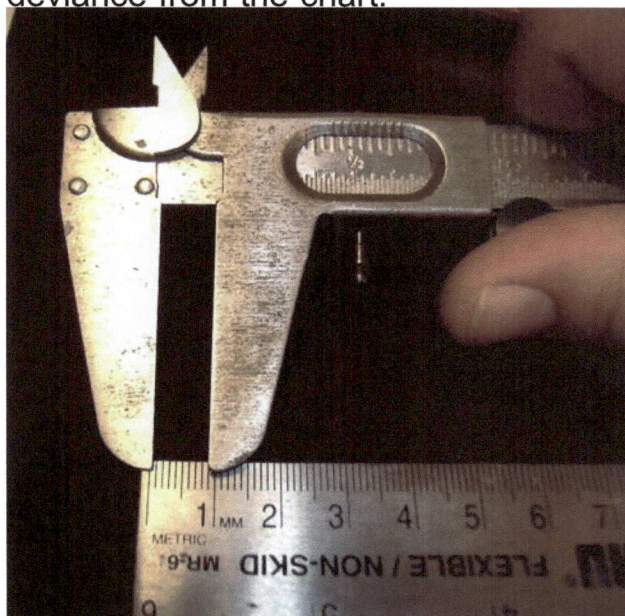

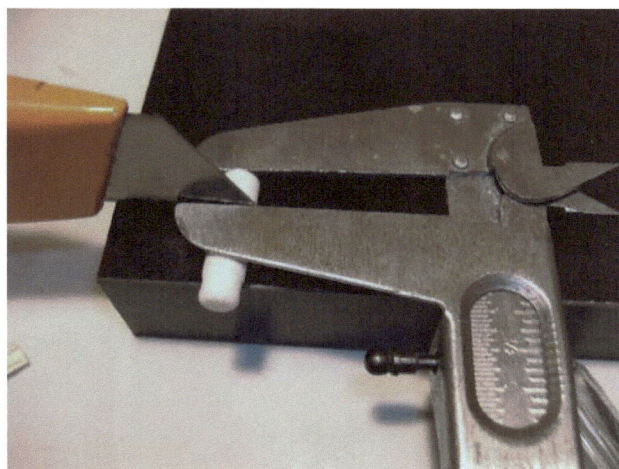

Step 8

I recommend using a pair of calipers similar to this one, placing the edge of the calipers at the top edge of the ruler to expose the markings on the (mm) millimeter scale. Go to the closest whole millimeter, and use your thumb on the adjuster wheel to go up or down slightly to get .25,.50,or .75 of a millimeter. A slight turn of the wheel will bring you as close as you need. Now you are ready to do the cutting. **NOW HERE IS THE TRICK-**The caliper has an uneven level in its lower adjustable jaw. Rest the edge of the eraser at the top of the jaw, and use the utility knife againts the lower jaws edge.The utility knife has a large enough blade that it can rest flat against the calipers jaw and give a straight cut. Make sure its positioned at the tables edge so the knife can come down completely. Make sure to number the markers as you cut, to the corrosponding number to the chart next to thier anotomical name.

TISSUE THICKNESS OF THE AMERICAN CAUCASOIDS (European derived)
All tables with permission and courtesy of Dr. Stan Rhine

MALE	Slender	NORMAL	Obese
1 Supraglabella	2.25	4.25	5.50
2 Glabella	2.50	5.25	7.50
3 Naion	4.25	6.50	7.50
4 Nasals end	2.50	3.00	3.50
5 Mid-philtrum	6.25	10.00	11.00
7 Lower lip	9.50	11.00	12.75
8 Chin-lip fold	8.75	10.75	12.25
9 Mental eminence	7.00	11.25	14.00
10 Beneath chin	4.50	7.25	10.75
11 Supraorbital	6.25	8.25	10.25
13 Sub Orbital	2.75	5.75	8.25
15 Lateral Orbit	5.00	10.00	13.75
16 Zygmatic arch half way	3.00	7.25	11.75
17 Supraglenoid	4.25	8.50	11.25
18 Gonion	4.50	11.50	17.50
20 Occusal line	12.00	18.25	23.50

FEMALE	Slender	Normal	Obese
1 supraglabella	2.50	3.50	4.25
2 Glabella	4.00	4.75	7.50
3 Naion	5.25	5.50	7.00
4 nasals end	2.25	2.75	4.25
5 mid-philtrum	5.00	8.50	9.00
7 lower lip	8.50	10.00	12.25
8 chin-lip fold	9.25	9.50	13.75
9 mental eminence	8.50	10.00	14.25
10 beneath chin	3.75	5.75	9.00
12 supraorbital	5.25	7.00	10.00
13 sub orbital	4.00	6.00	8.50
15 lateral orbit	6.00	10.75	14.75
16 zygmatic arch half way	3.50	7.50	13.00
17 supraglenoid	4.25	8.00	10.50
18 gonion	5.00	12.00	17.50
20 occusal line	11.00	17.00	20.25

TISSUE THICKNESS OF AMERICAN NEGROIDS (African derived)

MALE	Slender	Normal	Obese
1 supraglabella	4.00	5.00	5.00
2 Glabella	5.25	6.25	7.50
3 Nasion	5.25	6.00	5.25
4 nasals end	3.00	3.75	3.25
5 mid-philtrum	11.75	12.25	11.75
7 lower lip	13.75	15.50	15.50
8 chin-lip fold	11.75	11.75	13.00
9 mental eminence	11.25	11.50	15.25
10 beneath chin	8.00	8.25	9.50
12 supraorbital	7.75	8.50	11.75
13 sub orbital	5.75	7.75	9.25
15 lateral orbit	10.50	13.25	20.00
16 zygmatic arch half way	6.75	8.25	13.75
17 supraglenoid	9.50	11.00	17.50
18 gonion	11.50	13.00	24.00
20 occusal line	16.75	19.00	30.00

FEMALE	Slender	Normal	Obese
1 supraglabella	5.00	4.50	3.50
2 Glabella	6.00	6.00	6.00
3 Nasion	5.25	5.25	4.75
4 nasals end	3.25	3.75	3.00
5 mid-philtrum	10.00	11.25	12.00
7 lower lip	12.25	15.00	12.00
8 chin-lip fold	9.50	12.25	12.25
9 mental eminence	11.00	12.50	13.00
10 beneath chin	6.50	8.00	8.50
12 supraorbital	7.25	8.00	8.50
13 sub orbital	6.50	8.25	9.00
15 lateral orbit	12.00	13.00	12.75
16 zygmatic arch half way	8.00	9.50	9.25
17 supraglenoid	9.75	11.50	17.25
18 gonion	11.00	13.50	17.50
20 occusal line	17.25	19.25	20.00

It's time to glue down the markers. Use a glue that won't leave residue and a cement remover with acetone. For this project, use a gel cynoacrylate glue; it's known as a "super glue." Remember to read the directions and safety information on the container and don't get it on your skin. You can use kid's model glue for this project if preferable. As always, be careful when gluing the markers.

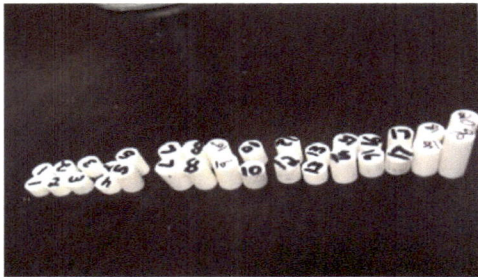

The cut markers.

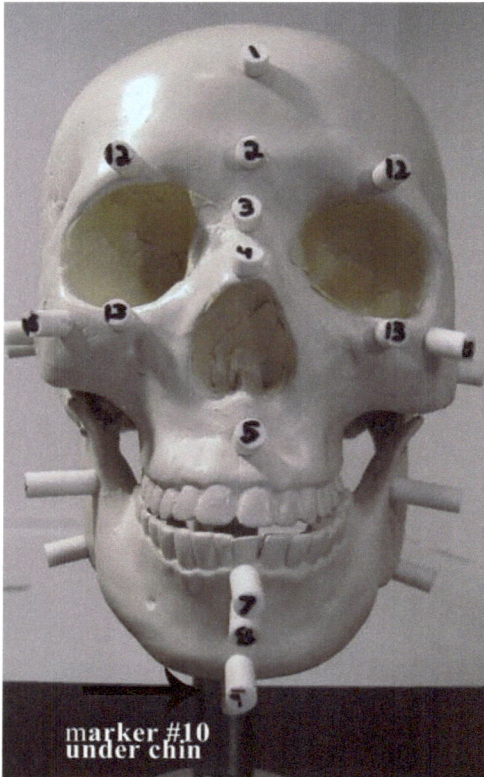

Step 9 continued
The red line shows that the skull is "level" on the stand, this avoids distortion. The "Frankfort Horizontal Plane" is the line from the lowest part of the eye socket, to the ear hole. This is how to level the skull.

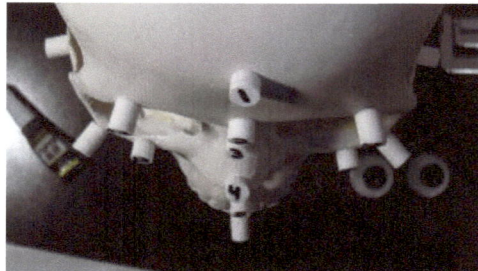

marker #10 under chin

Step 9
Glue on the markers. #10 is under the chin and not visible from this angle.

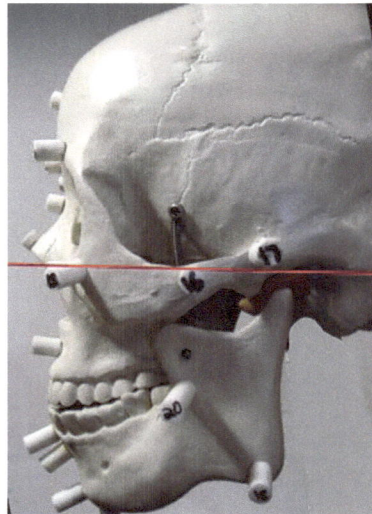

It is normal for the markers to not be placed in an even pattern over the skull, the skull it self is not perfectly even.

Look carefully at the marker placement. Notice on the model there are areas that look carved. This comes from the molding process. On the more expensive skulls, such marks cannot be found. It is proper for markers on each side of the skull not to be in the exact same spot, our faces are asymmetrical.

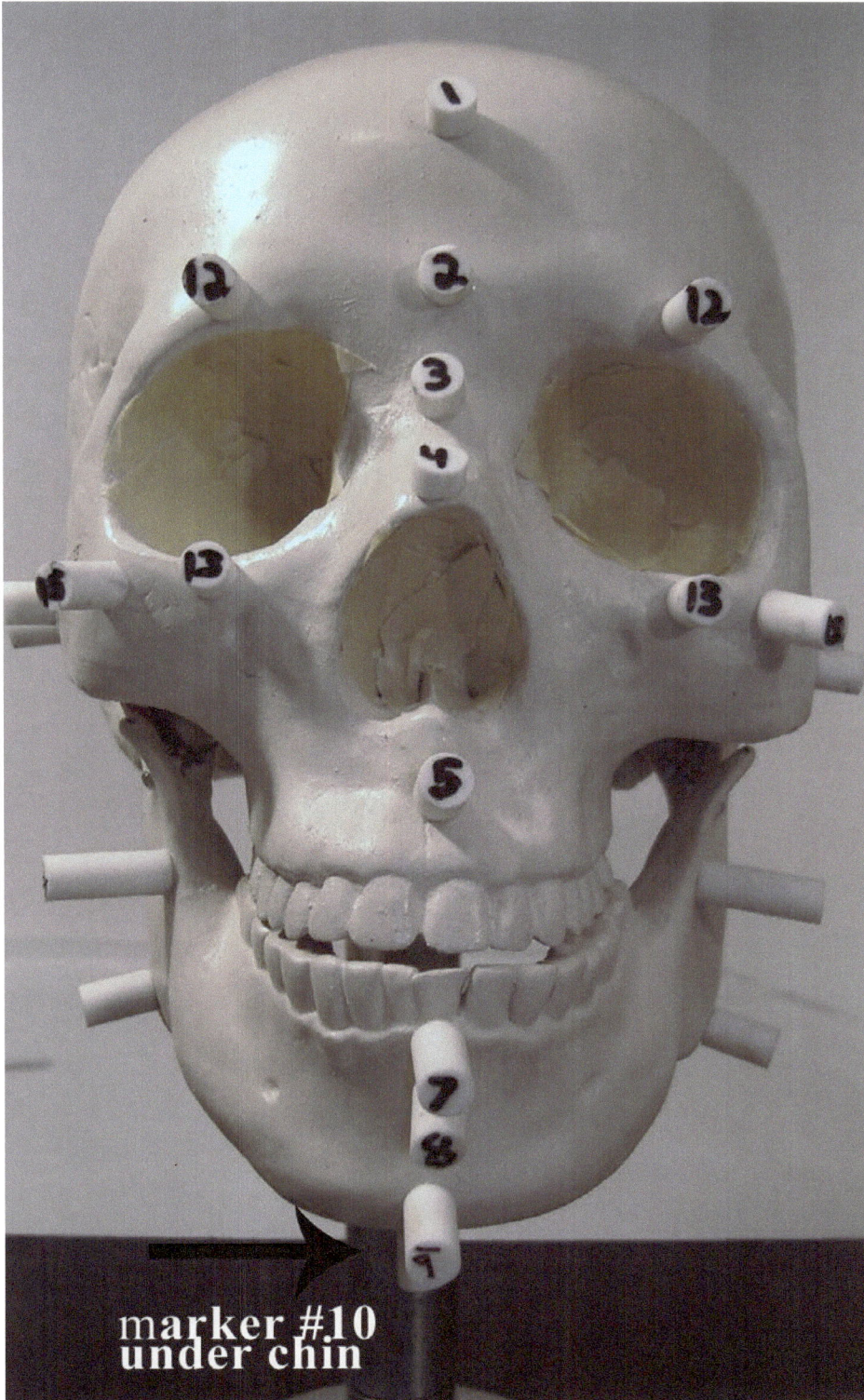

marker #10
under chin

Notice marker #17 and the clay spacer at the jaw. This is also the time to make sure the skull is level on the pipe. On a real skull glue the jaw to the skull with a space of a few Millimeters, you can space it with clay then glue it carefully. Be extremely careful with a real skull.

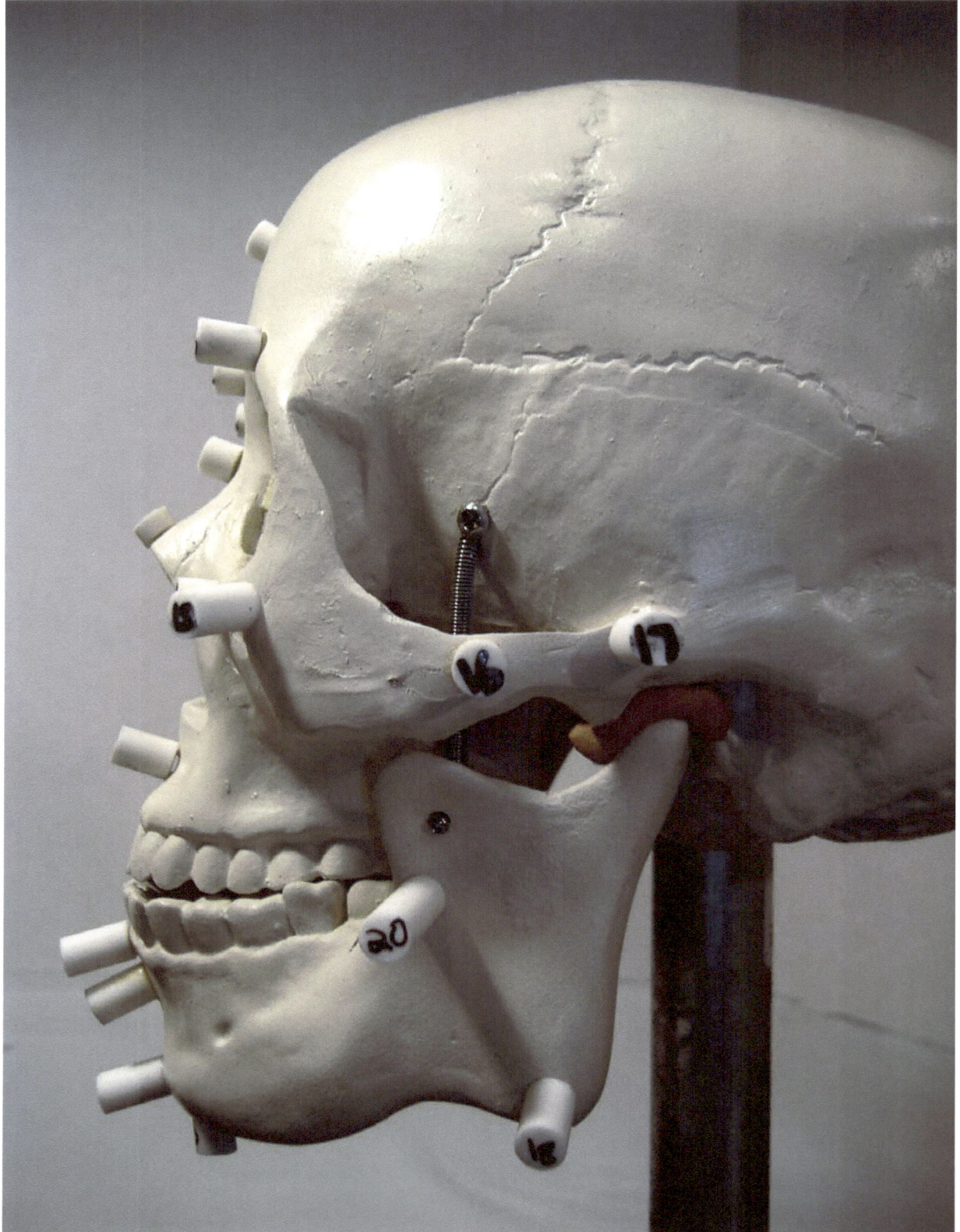

PART SEVEN: EYES AND NECK

Step 10
Use clay to secure the neck and skull in the horizontal position. Allow some room to make a small neck.

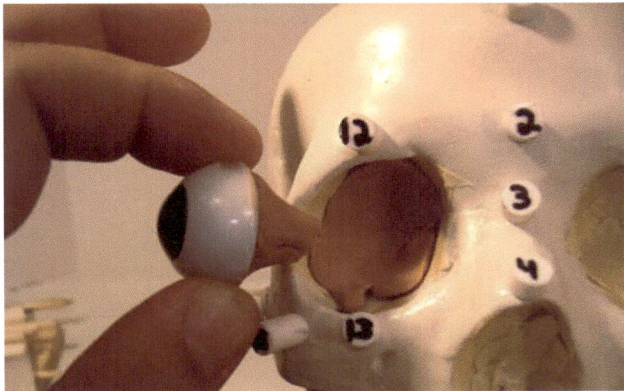

Step 11
Use a nutcracker to CAREFULLY remove the back of the plastic eyes so as not to damage the eyes or pinch your fingers. I must note that plastic eyes are only good for practice. I recommend using glass eyes or medical prosthetic eyes. The eyes will be *THE* feature that give your sculpture life. I recommend going with light brown or brown eyes when hair color is not known. Place a bit of clay in the socket and on the back of the eye to hold in place.

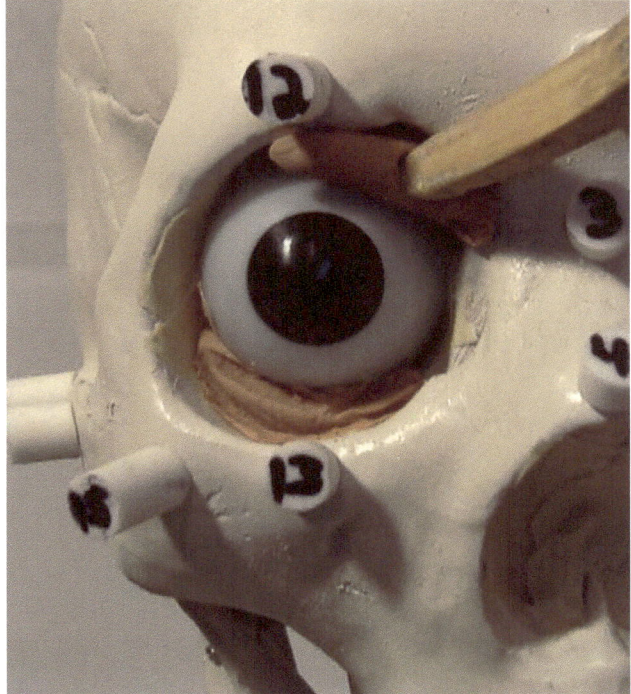

Step 12
To set the eye, **center the pupil**. Then use a wooden tool and clay to secure it. Notice that the eyes are not round but have a raised, dome-like pupil. Never use a metal tool on glass or plastic eyes because it will scratch them.

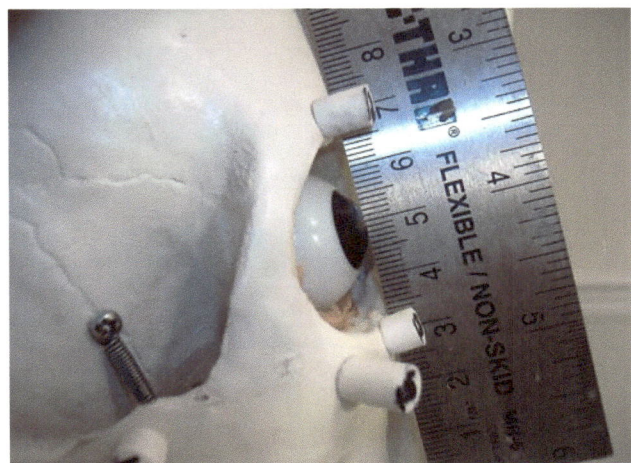

Step 13
Use the flat edge of the ruler against the skull and against the pupil. That will set them to the correct depth.

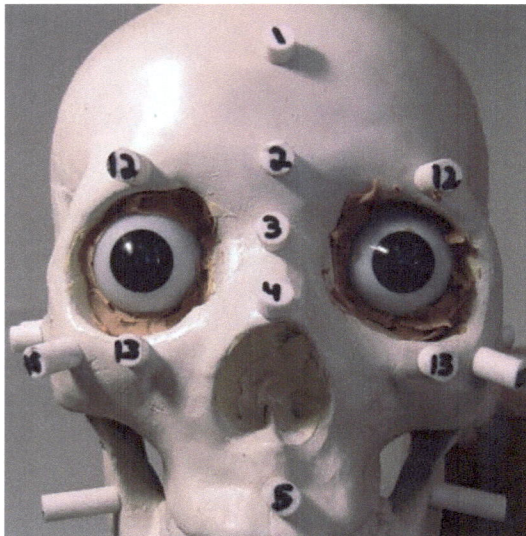

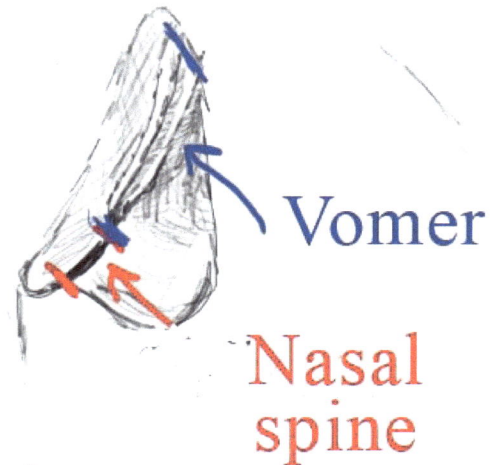

Vomer

Nasal spine

Step 14
Set the second eye! This is the hardest yet most important part to the entire process. First secure one eye so it looks straight ahead. If it's staring off in one direction, it's okay. This will infuse life and feeling into the sculpture. Next, place the other eye, and do your best to match it. The trick is to check your work in a mirror. When looking in a mirror, the perspective is different as opposed to looking at the sculpture straight on. You can also use a digital camera's back screen. Take your time and look from all angles.

Ours is 7mm. The nasal spine is the tip of the spine to the vomer. It'is not always apparent on real skulls. It can be broken or missing, so you may need to make an educated guess. This is why the nose can be so difficult to recreate.On the other hand, the nose, when measured properly, can be incredibly accurate.

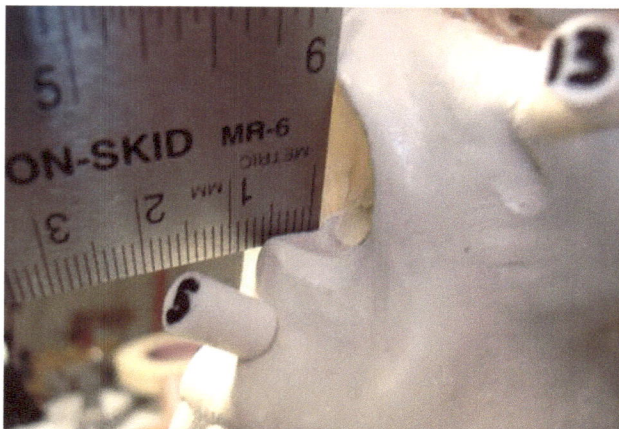

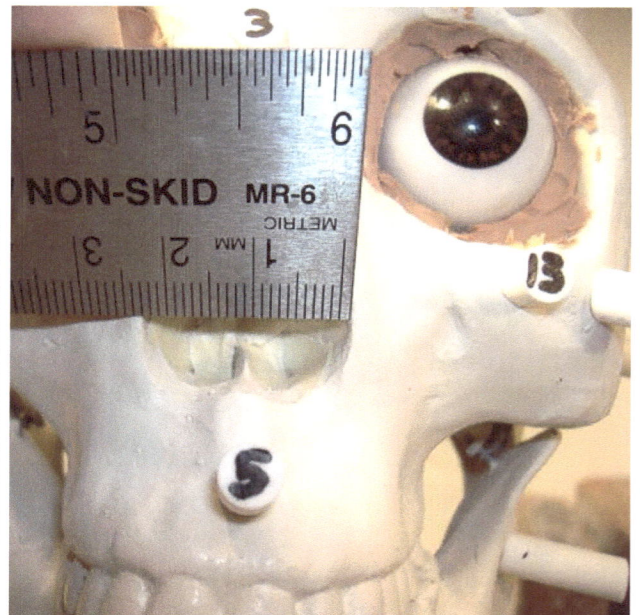

PART EIGHT: FORMULAS
Step 15
Measure the anterior nasal spine.

Step 16
Measure the width of the nose at its widest point. Ours is 25mm.

FORMULAS TO MAKE THE NOSE AND MOUTH

Do this now before you begin. It's better to put this on paper before the clay is molded over the skull.

31mm

Nasal spine x 3+Marker#5=length

ours

7x3=21+10=31

DOUBLE CHECK THESE YOURSELF.

35mm

caucasoids = 10mm (5mm on each side as nostrils) + Width
Negroids = 16mm (8 on each side as nostrils) + width
OURS
25mm (width) + 10mm = 35mm

FORMULAS TO MAKE THE LIPS

First, remove the #7 marker from the skull. It doesn't need to be attached.

#7 marker = thickness
space between ridge on upper and lower teeth = height
outside edge of canine to outside edge of canine = width

height = space
between enamel
and root of
upper and lowers

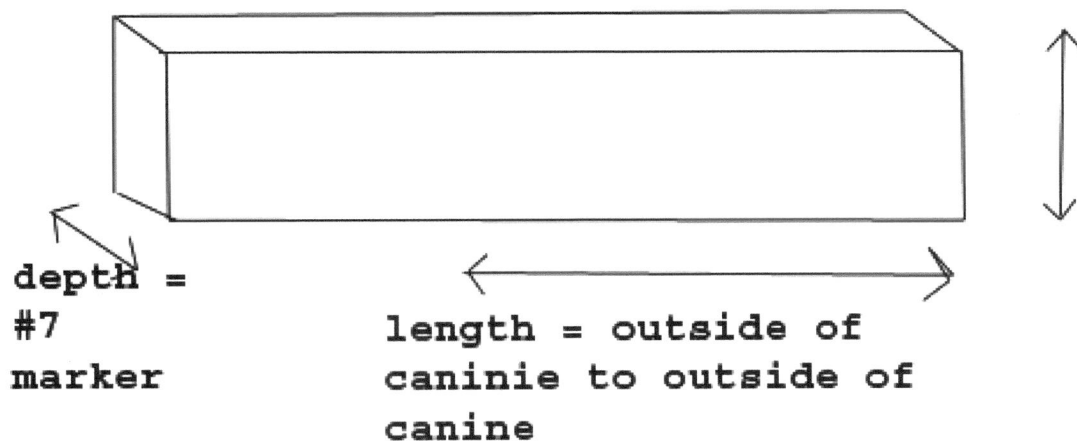

depth =
#7
marker

length = outside of
caninie to outside of
canine

Here is an example of what to look for when measuring the lip hieght. The area where the root ends and the enamel begins have a very slight ridge. Measure from ridge to ridge. It may be necessary to hold the skull in different lighting or even feel the area with your fingertips.

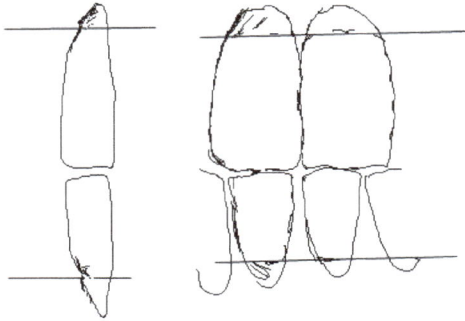

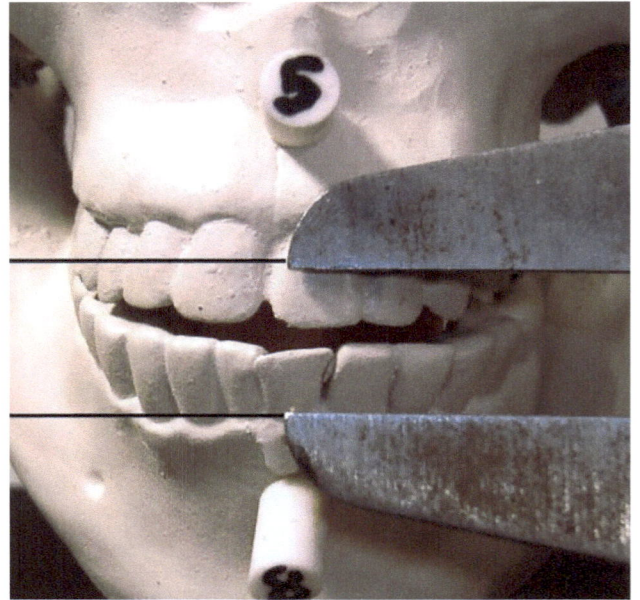

.

height = space
between enamel
and root of
upper and lowers

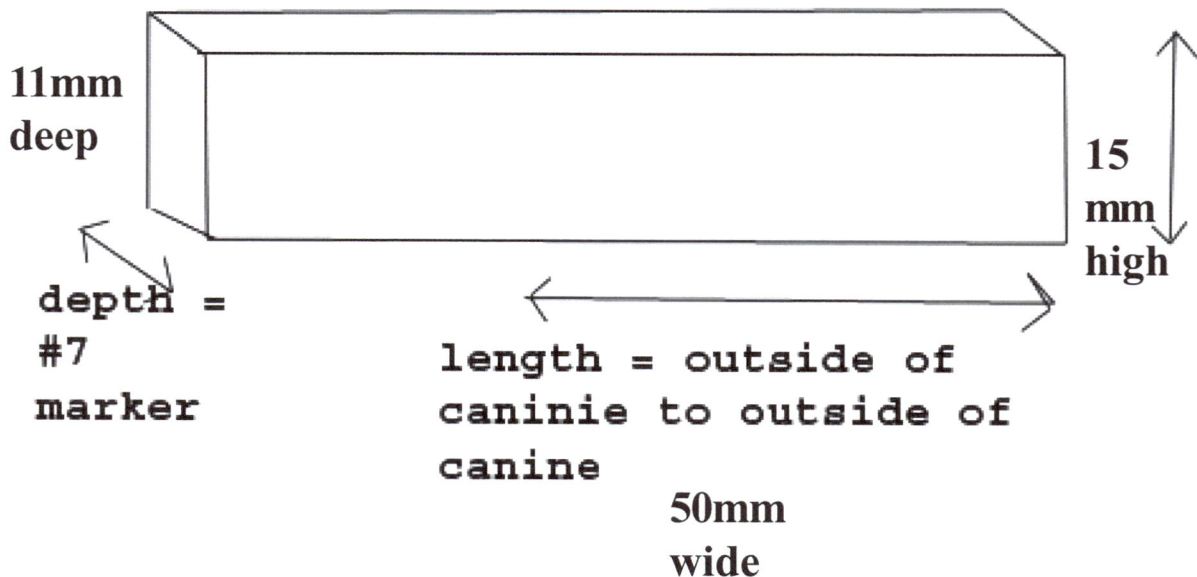

11mm
deep

15
mm
high

depth =
#7
marker

length = outside of
caninie to outside of
canine

50mm
wide

PART NINE: TIME TO CUT THE CLAY AND START THE SCULPTURE!

There are different methods to making slabs of clay the appropriate thickness to the corresponding marker. You can use a roller, a rolling pin, or I prefer using either an adjustable cheese cutter or making a clay rolling board like you see below. To do that, take popsicle sticks, or dowels and measure thier height. Then, glue them on a board 1/2" apart. I have mine at 4 and 5mm thick. This is so I can roll out and double clay from 4mm to 8mm, and 5mm to 10mm thick. I will use the cheese slicer for other measurements. If I need to get to ¼ or ½ of a Mm. I will roll a slightly thicker piece down to the size I need. Then put clay between the dowels and roll it into the shape like you see here. Take your time. You must do this right or you will not get the proper thickness, which subsequently, will not result in a realistic, true-to-form sculpture.

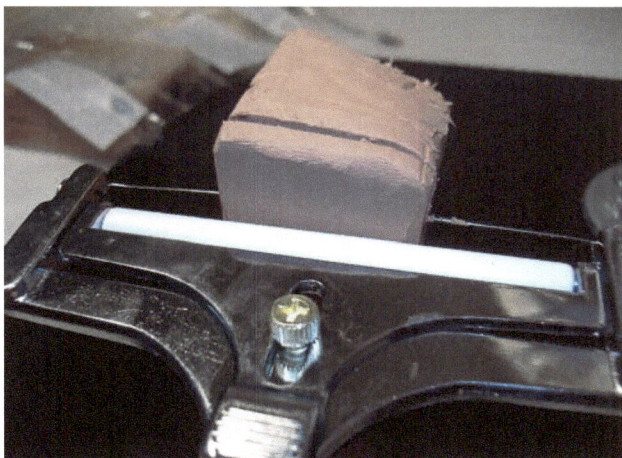

Step 17
Cut the clay with either a cheese slicer or use a clay board pictured below. Glue the popsickle sticks or dowels to a wooden cutting board or plywood with superglue to create a board as seen below.

Lay down plastic wrap over the clay board when using. Then put clay in the area you want to use and more plastic wrap over that. This helps prevent clay from sticking to the rolling pin.

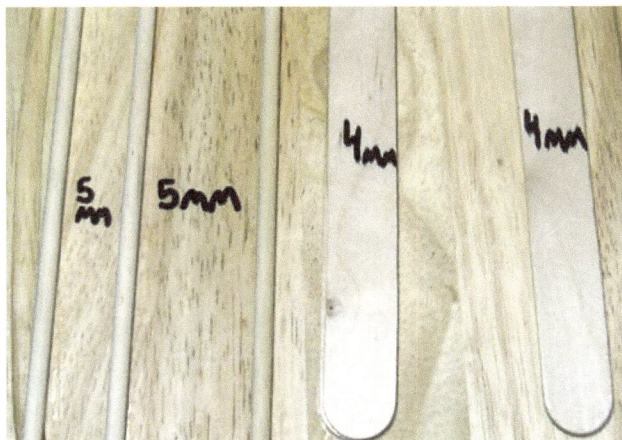

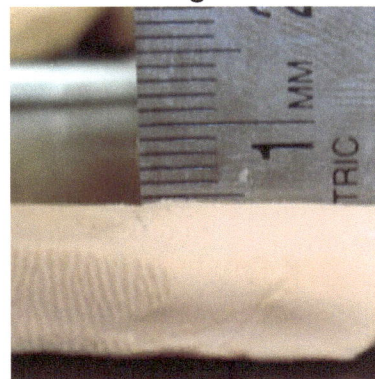

When you begin making the slabs, use the cheese slicer as seen in the photo above left, or use the clay rolling board as pictured at the top right. Notice that I have an even 5mm thick slab of clay!

When placing clay on the skull, remember to be accurate. You may have to add or subtract clay when connecting to other markers. Do so gradually so there is never a divet, just a smooth transition.

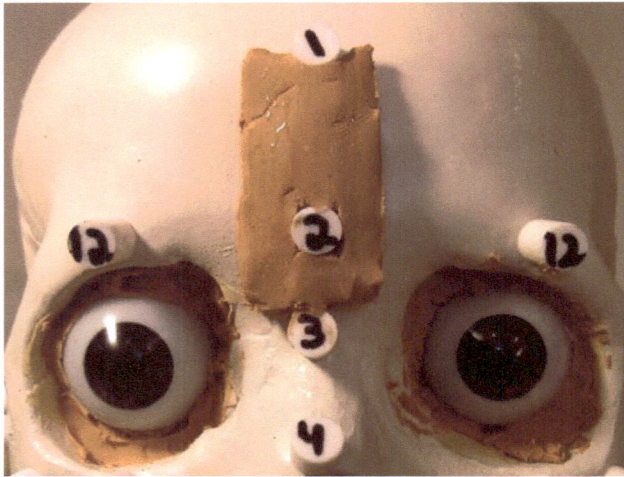

Step 18
Marker 1 to 3. Roll out the clay to the size of marker 1 and connect it to the top of marker three as seen above. Make sure there is a smooth transition, around marker 2.

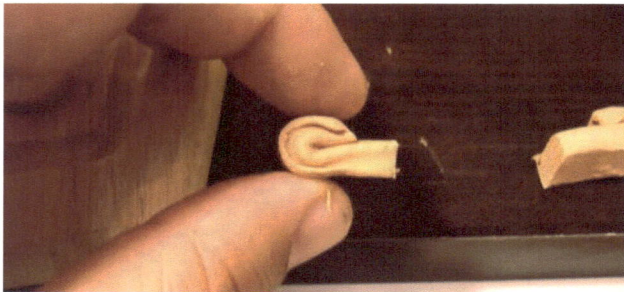

Step 19
Marker 3 to 12. Roll out the thickness for marker 1 and fold over the ends that will go next to marker 12. This will make the transition easier.

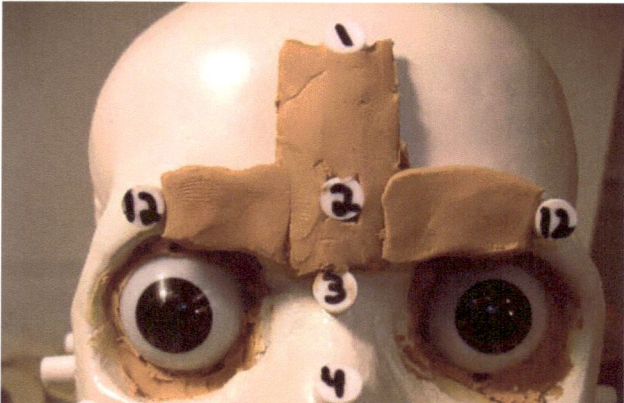

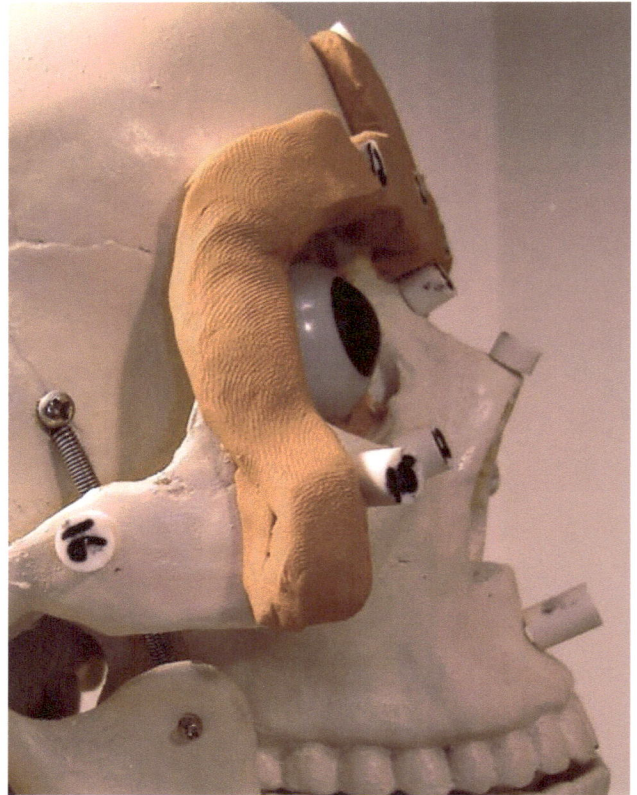

Step 20
Marker 12 to behind 15. As in the previous strip, fold over one end, and then this time the other end, both about 3 or 4 mm. The area beside the eye needs to stay thin. Now you can connect 12 to 15. As in the side view above, and front view below.

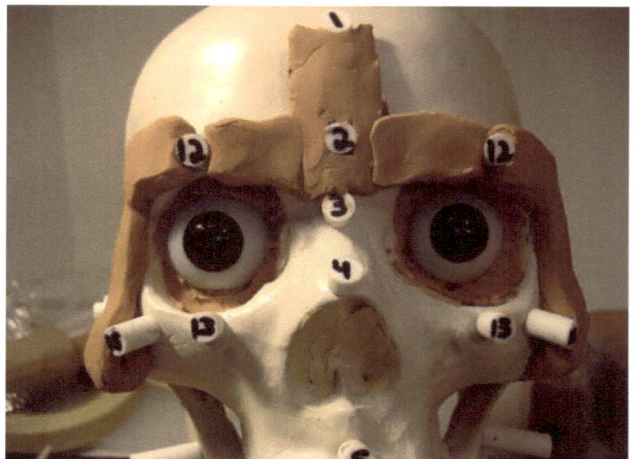

Step 21
Markers 15,16,17,18 and 20. THE CLAY TRIANGLE! Place pieces of clay in this area and slowly build up until it's filled and smooth as shown below. Make sure there are no divets. Follow the curve at the back of the jaw.

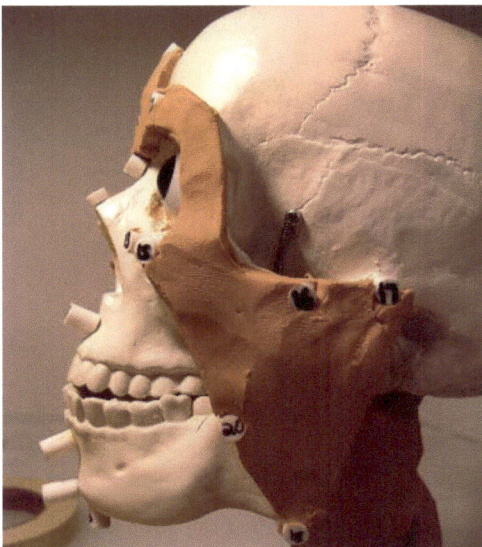

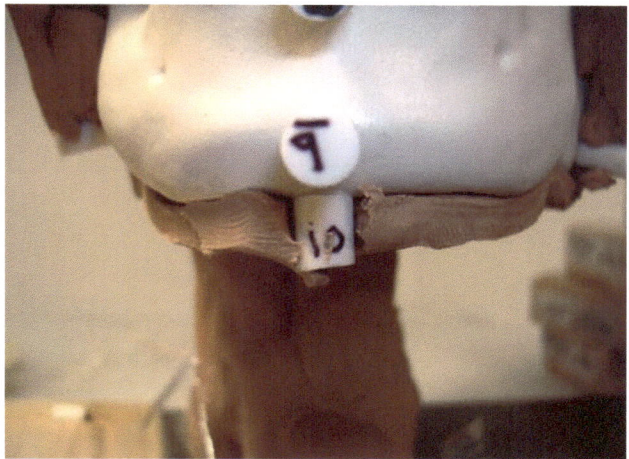

Step 22
Marker 18 to 10. This is where the cheese slicer works ideally for long strips. Follow underneath the jaw.

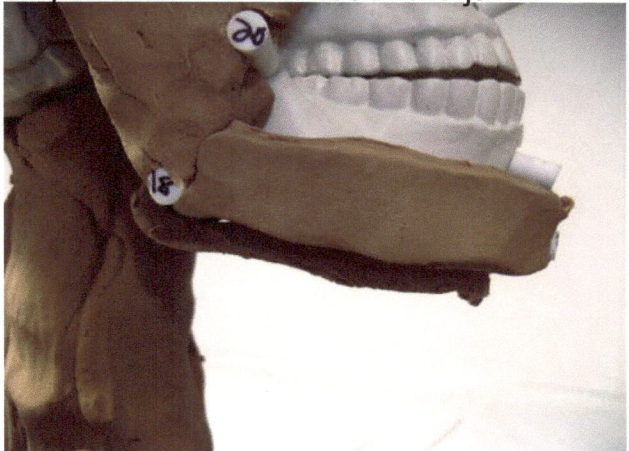

Step 23
Marker 18 to 9. Again, I used the slicer to make a great long slab here.

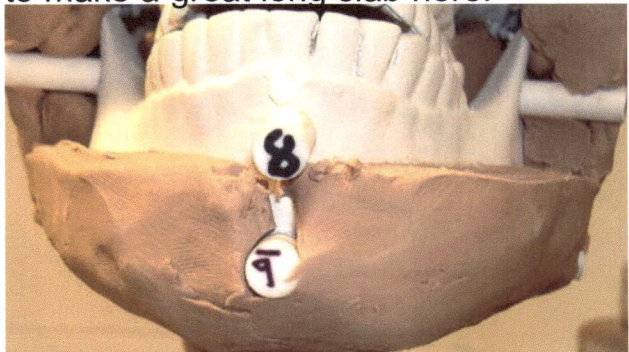

Step 24
Blend the two together to make seamless.

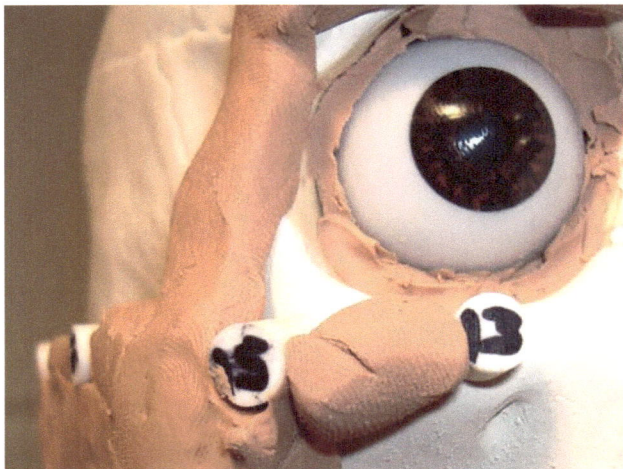

Step 25
Connect marker 15 to 13.

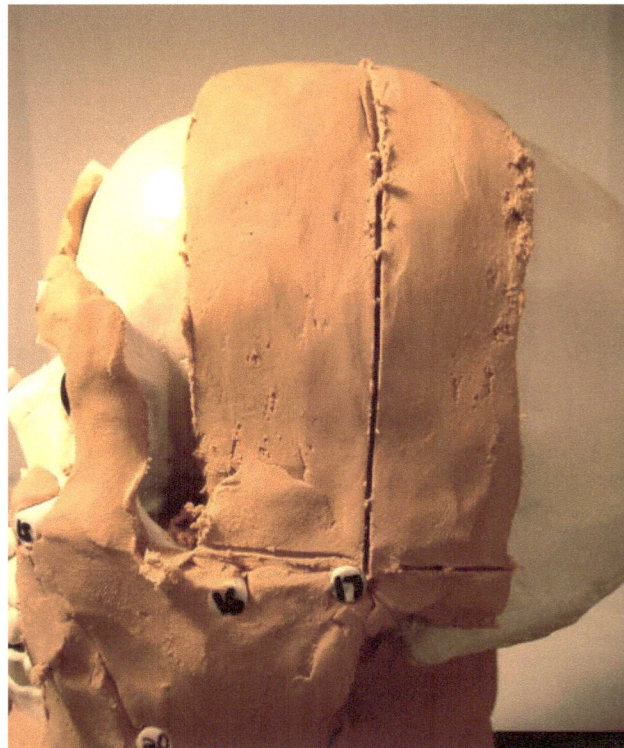

Step 26
Marker 13 to jaw. Now add clay from 13 down to the jaw, centered between 18 and 9. Measure between markers 18 and 19 to find the center of the jaw, as shown.

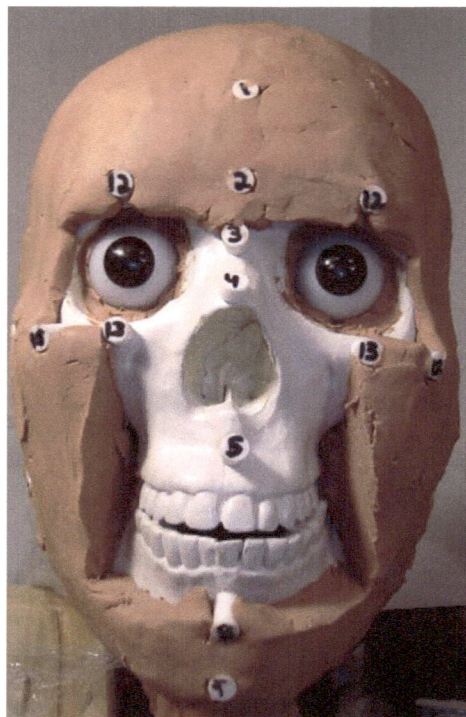

Step 27
Roll out wide slabs on your clay board the thickness of marker 1 and lay them from the forehead back.

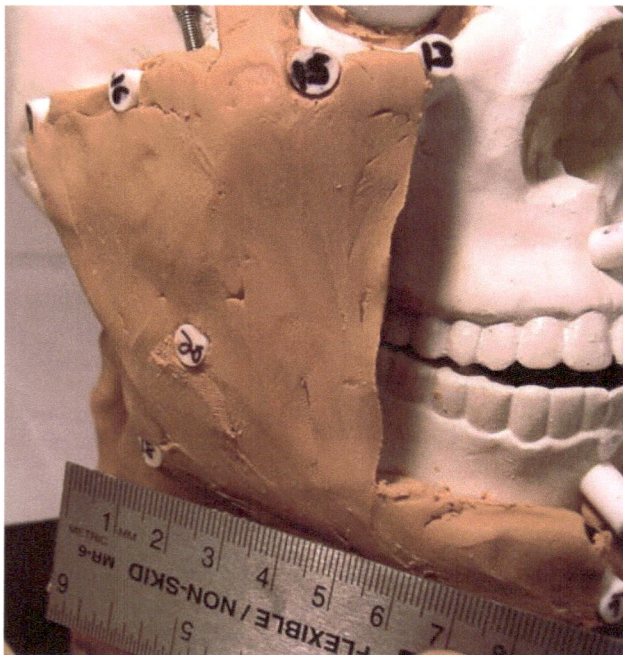

Smoothed and ready for the next phase.

PART TEN: SCULPTING

When sculpting, always maintain the same level of detail as you progress along. In other words, don't put skin texture on one side or smooth large sections until everything is actually ready to be smoothed. If you don't work evenly, those areas will end up needing to be reworked anyway. It's much harder to match one side to another that is already complete. This results in getting stuck in one spot, resculpting in the detail over and again. Remember that both sides of the face don't have to be exactly the same, just *extremely similar*. Be careful not to sculpt *your* own features on the sculpture. Most sculptors tend to put their own nose or mouth or chin on a sculpture.

Now it's time to begin sculpting the mouth. For this we will first discuss sculpting, the tools, and what they are for. Each tool has a specific purpose. The first tool - and the one that should never be used unless necessary - are your fingers. Using your hands is acceptable for laying down large areas as well as placing bits of clay to help in the first part of the project. However, at this point, it's recommended to use specific tools for each step.

The second tool is a wooden or plastic "blade" tool. They almost look like wooden butter knives. These are good for pushing clay into corners, spreading, and connecting clay sections. I use this to place my eye lids and other areas. There are tools that are basically just thin, dull knives that are good for cutting clay, but be careful because they can be dangerous.

My favorite tool is the loop tool. Which is used to cut into and shave clay, they are great for shaping the eyelids and carving the nostrils. Large ones carve whole clay figures. These tools are the most versatile. You can create realistic folds and wrinkle with them.

The last tool mentioned here are the detail tools. Some have little balls on the end of a pin and some are just pins. They are basically dental tools. These can be found cheap at flea markets. Expensive ones can be found in art stores. The less pricey ones are preferable, however they should still be of a good quality. Some other tools to be used are sponges, such as red and black "stipple" sponges from a make-up fx supply store. These create great skin texture, though plastic food wrap and dental tools are better. The latter route is much slower, but it's worth it. This method is shown within these pages, but will be more fully demonstrated in the upcoming make-up fx book series.

Finally, there are the solvents. Use the solvents on the appropriate clays with a "stencil brush" to smooth out the clay. These brushes can actually sculpt the clay. There is another type of sculpting tool that I have not used, though I believe also works wonderfully: the "eraser" tool. These have wooden handles with a silicone rubber tip.They are really for charcoal drawing. Take notice of the tools used in each step's photo, especially how they are held to achieve better results.

Never stop practicing sculpting. Buy books and videos, or take classes. You must continue learning and honing your craft. Once you realize that we never really "pay our dues" you will be able to always grow as an artist and professional. In all of my years teaching and working with others, I am always learning something new. The best methods usually come from mistakes students made that I did not think were possible. Make sure to be helpful to everyone who asks, you will get more jobs in the long run by helping people. You will get the jobs you want if you have the right skills.

To develop your attention to detail, start a reference file. Compile good close-up photo's of people's faces - young, old, whatever. Look for textures. Also keep in mind that this is just clay. If you drop it, bump it, smash it, or mash it, it's only clay and can be reworked. Even though you won't enjoy starting over, it will be a great chance to do a better job.

When you are creating a forensic sculpture, protocols usually require you to remove the clay soon after photographing or after the trial so the skull can be buried. Don't despair - you will always have your pictures. Make sure that everything is photographed - the good and the bad - so you can look back critically and learn from your work. This is why i recommend good photographic equiptment. The key to masterful sculpting is to keenly observe the subject from every angle, above, below, and so on. Look at your sculpture from those angles too. Use a mirror to observe facial features - the way an eye curves, how much iris shows in an eye. Facing your sculpture into the mirror and looking at its reflection, you discern many common mistakes and can then fix them. Make sure to clean the skull completely and carefully when you finish.

With that I will empart an obvious yet important tip worth saying: make sure that your next sculpture is as good as or better than the last.

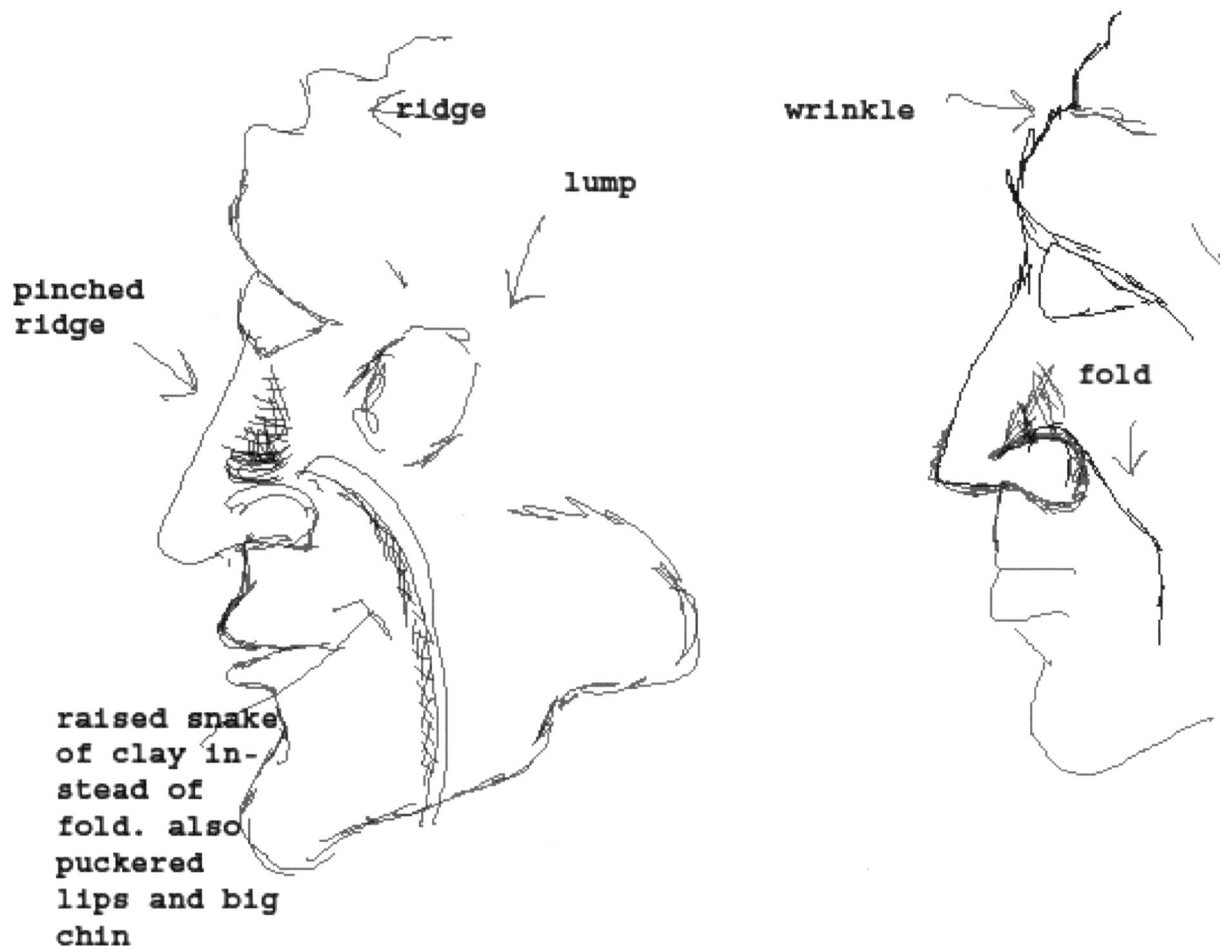

ridge

lump

pinched
ridge

raised snake
of clay in-
stead of
fold. also
puckered
lips and big
chin

wrinkle

fold

This rendering is full of bad mistakes. The cheek bone is a lump pinched at the top and the bridge of the nose is pinched. The forehead has ridges similar to an grotesque alien. The lips are pursed and the chin is oversized. The nasal fold is a raised snake of clay on top of the cheek. In sum, don't use your fingers!

This one is correct. The fold is the cheek folded over the mouth. The forehead has wrinkles and the nostril is lower at the back than the front. Remember that your tear duct is lower than the outer corner to let tears roll out.

PART ELEVEN: MOUTH

This phase is going to utilize the math we went over earlier. It's recommended that you redo all of the math, mine and yours. Take your time. Now, roll out the slabs the thickness of marker 7. Then cut it the height which is obtained from the enamel/root levels. Finally, obtain the width from the space between the outsides of each canine tooth (they are the "pointy vampire teeth" we all have.)

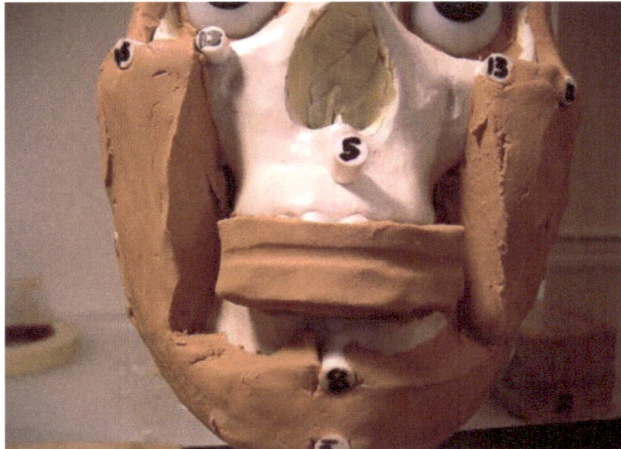

Step 28
Place your mouth from outside canine to outside, which is about 6 teeth wide.

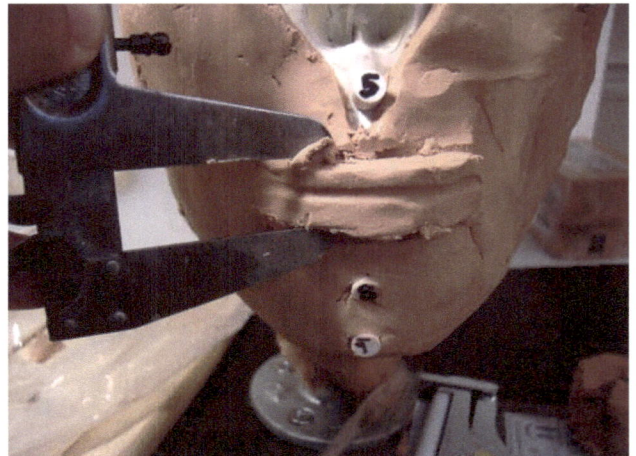

Step 29
Roll out and lay down clay from 13 to the top of the mouth. Cut the bottoms of the strips to lie against the upper lip.

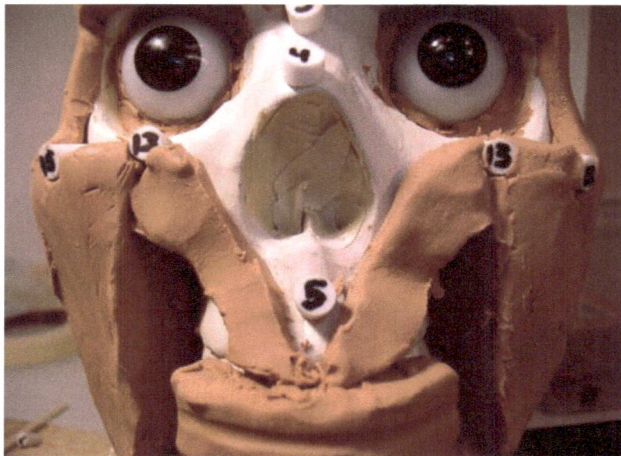

Step 30
Fill in the area around the mouth and re-check your mouth measurements. You can use the calipers to sculpt the size back in. Now, refrigerate the head for at least one hour.

With a real skull, you should just put it in a cool room. This will make the next steps easier. You may want to turn up your air conditioner.

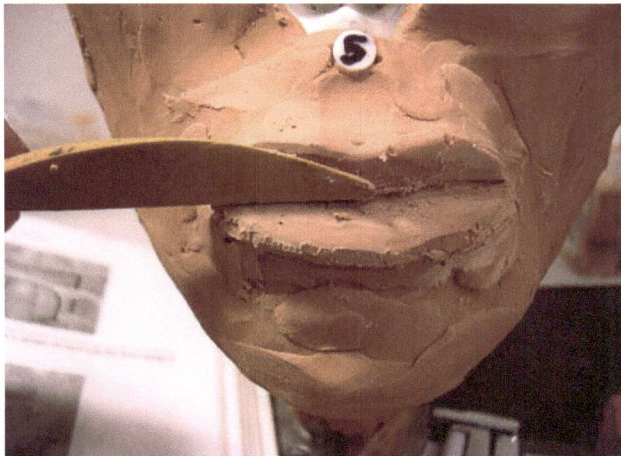

You can see I added the muscles that are below the corners of the mouth.

Step 30 continued
Use your wooden or plastic blade to press the lip into a rough shape. Then use your loop tool to achieve a more defined shape.

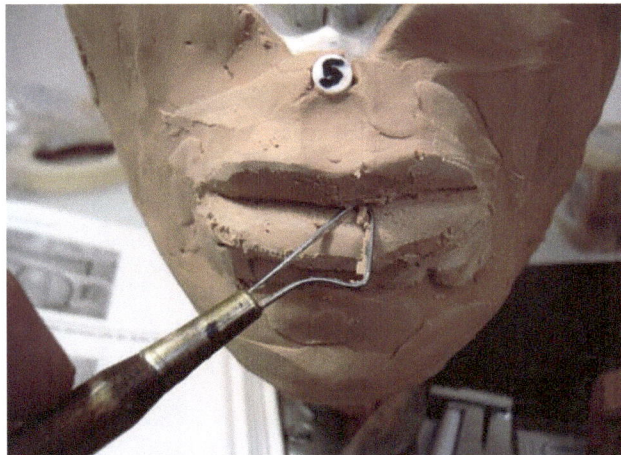

Don't forget to study the mouth to see how the lower lip folds under the top lip. Look at how I hold the tool, angled on its side and dragging it lightly. You can always take off more. Then when the lips are roughed out you can put in the dip over the top lip. Avoid sculpting ridges when creating wrinkles or folds. Many tend to make ridges on the forehead instead of wrinkles. Ask the question "does this look real?" or "does it look alien?"

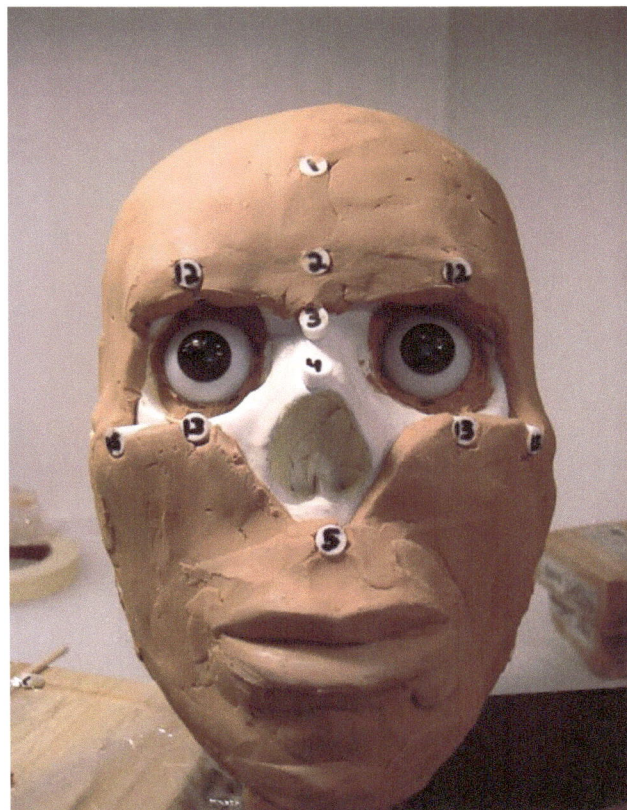

PART TWELVE: EYELIDS

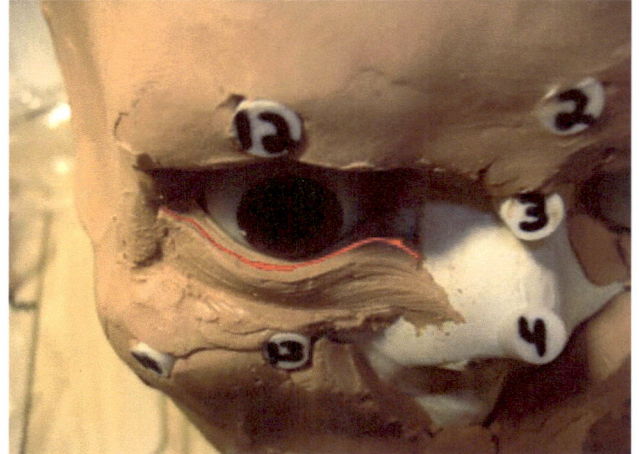

This is the shape you want.

Step 31
Create a lower lid by making a piece 3mm thick and about 7mm long. Create an "s" shape with the strip.

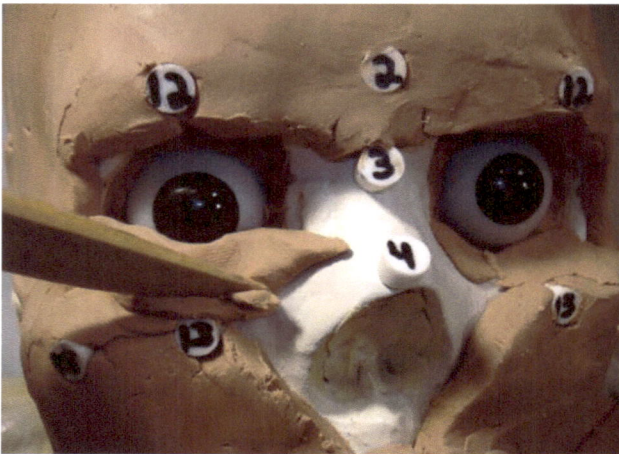

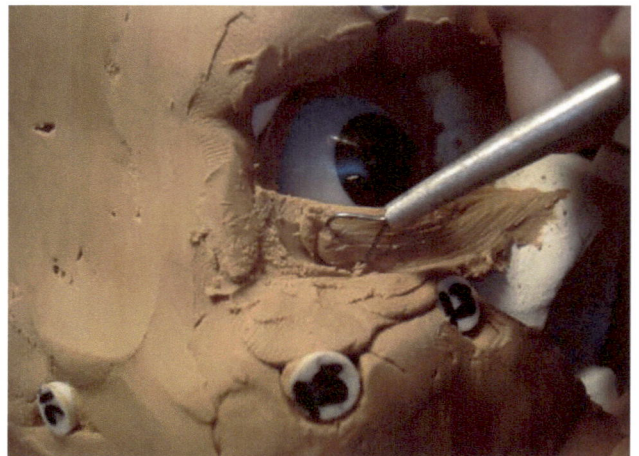

Use a wooden tool for this. Lay it from the outer corner of the eye to the inner corner at the nose. Make sure the inner corner that will be the tear duct, is lower than the outside corner.

To get good form, use your thin loop tool. Keep it tilted at a 45 degree angle top edge going out from the eye like the picture demonstrates. Your lower lid goes under the eyeball. Take your time and use a mirror and reference photos.

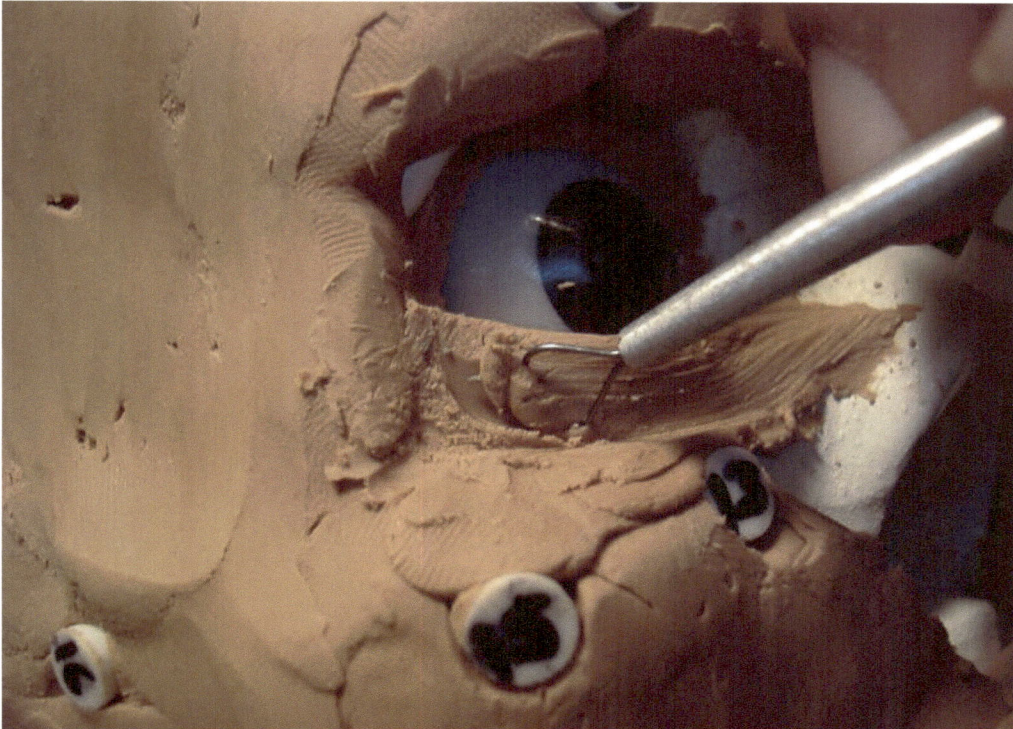

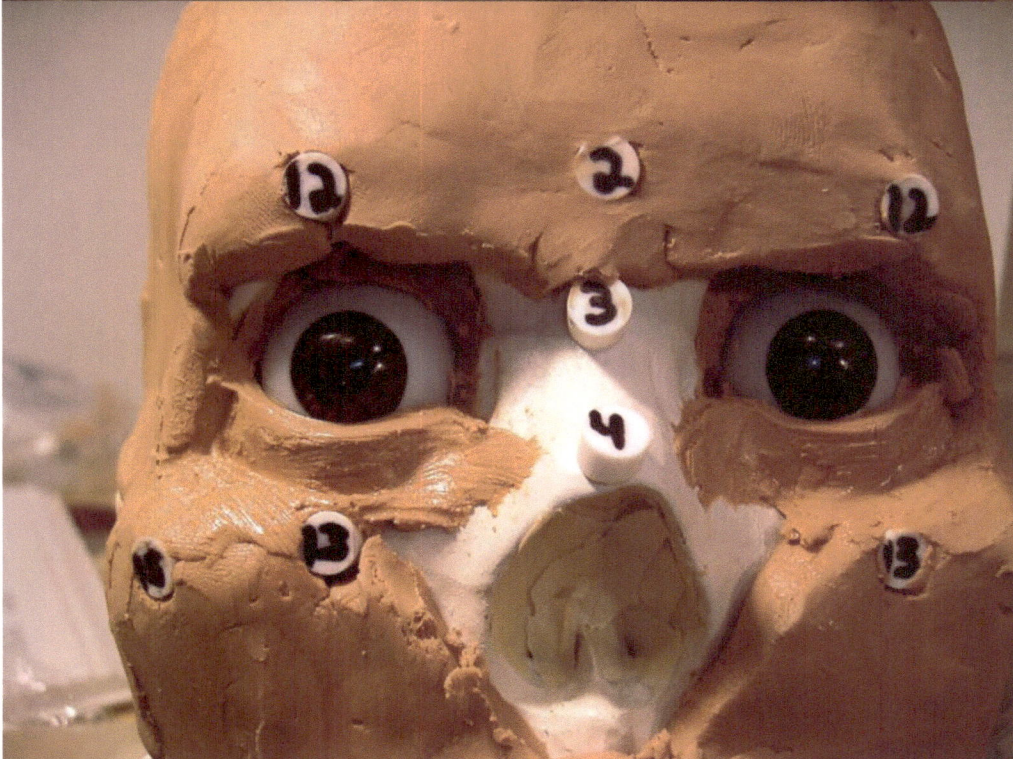

This is a good shape for the lower lids. I used alcohol to smooth the clay.

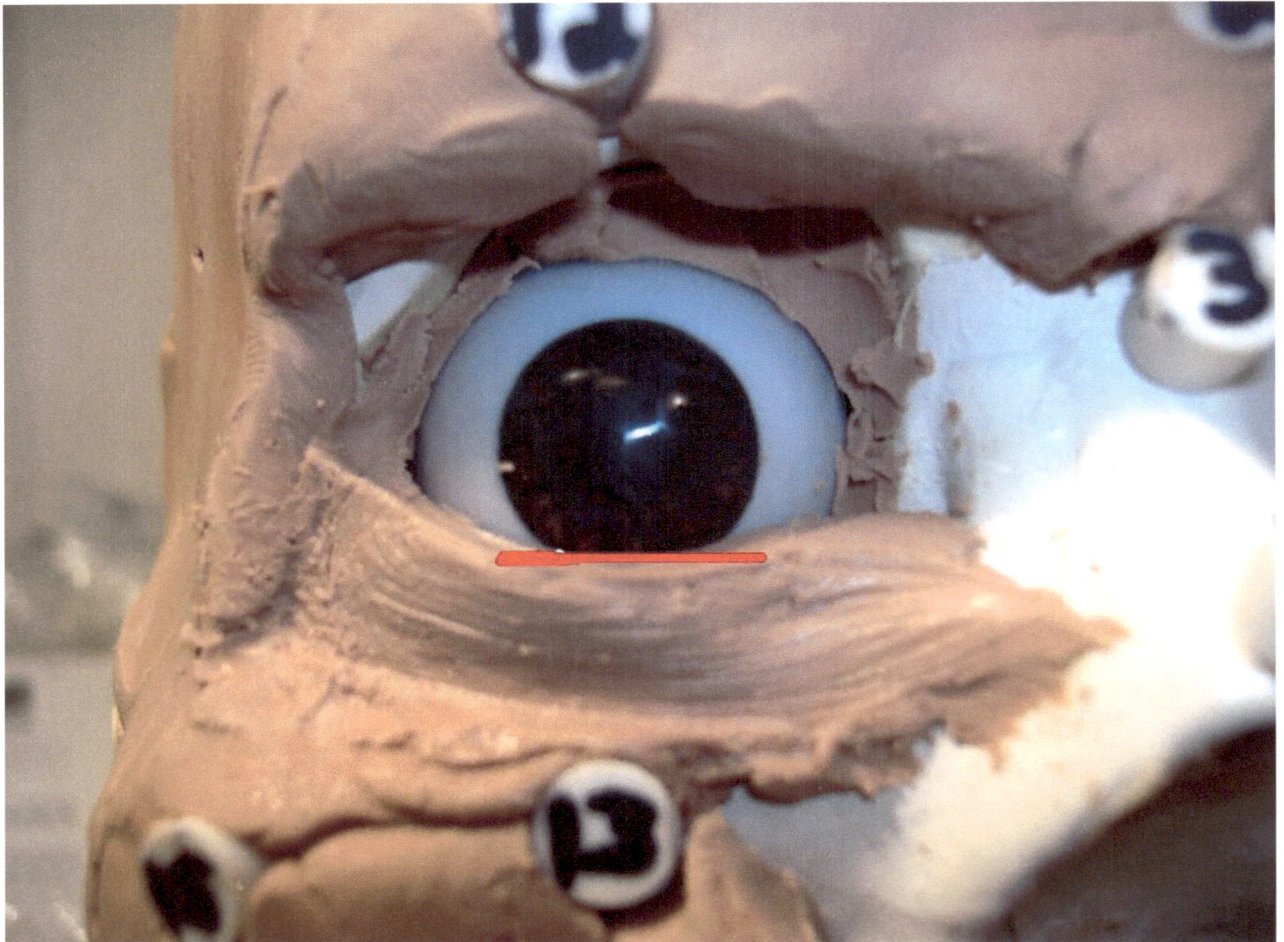

Look at your own eye in the mirror to see where the iris rests!

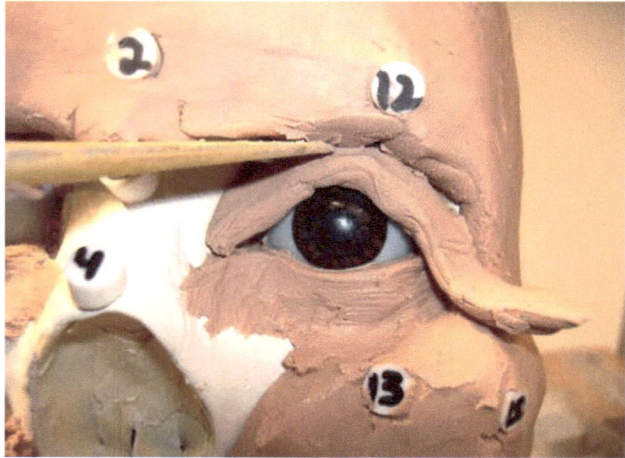

Step 32
Use your wooden tool and some similar strips to create the upper lid.

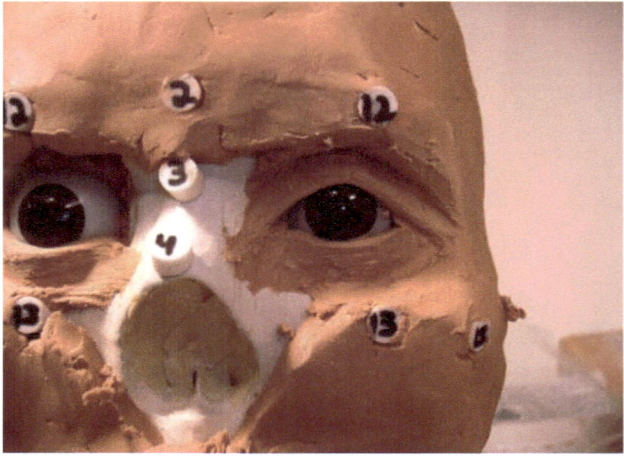

The upper and lower lids together.

STEP 33

Add the muscle above your eye, about 5mm thick. Add more if needed.

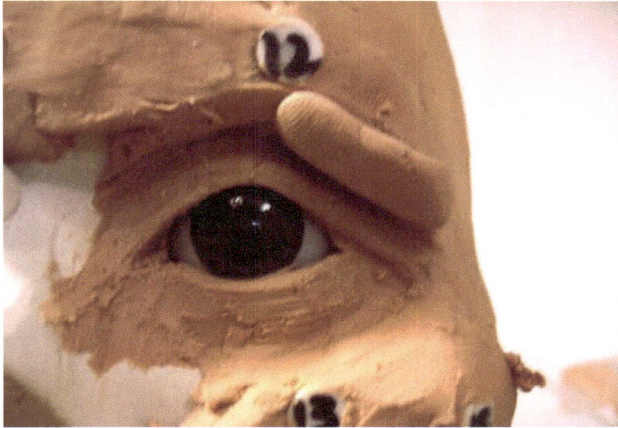

PART THIRTEEN: THE NOSE

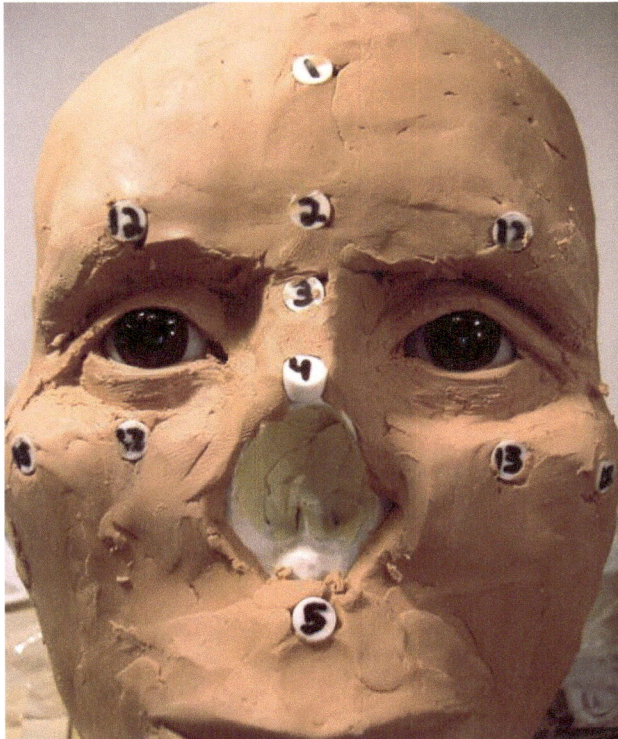

This is where you should be now. At this point, look over your work and review every step. Being methodical minimizes the chance of having to redo anything major towards the end of your sculpture.

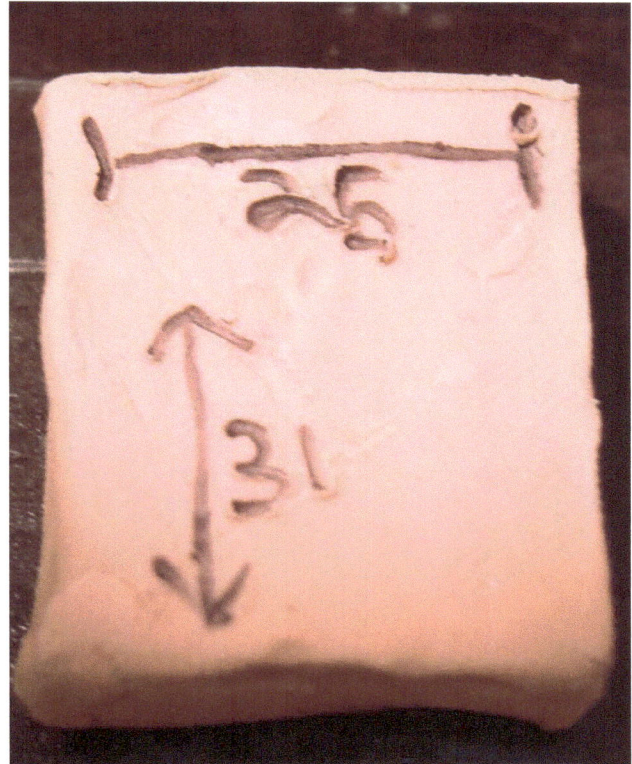

Step 34

Cut the brick from your nose measurements. Leave off the 10mm that will eventually be the nostrils.

Watch the angle when you place it. It goes right over the top edge of marker 5. Follow the angle of the nasal spine. This helps tell if the nose turns up or down.

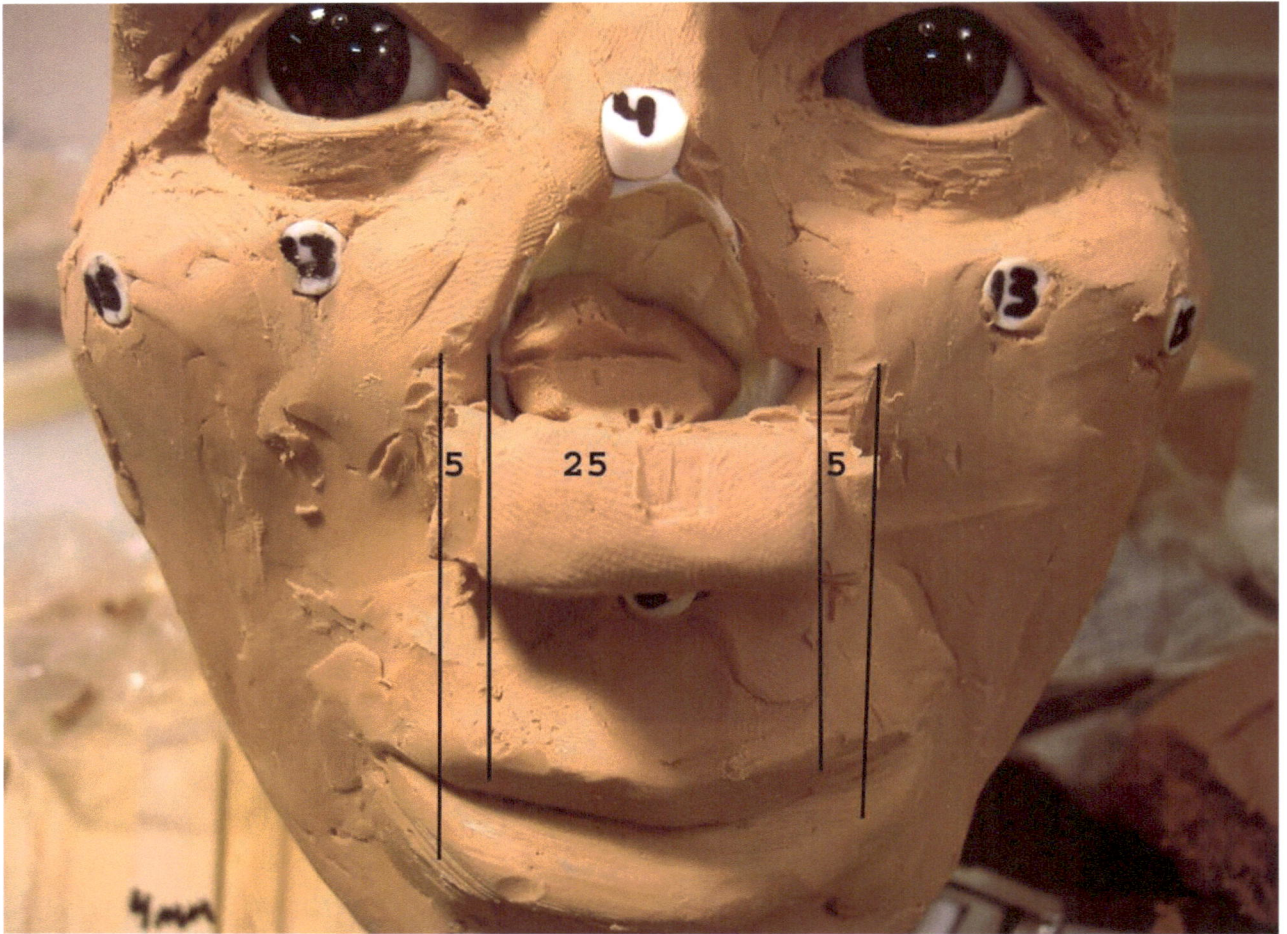

Step 35
Add your nostrils and check your measurements.

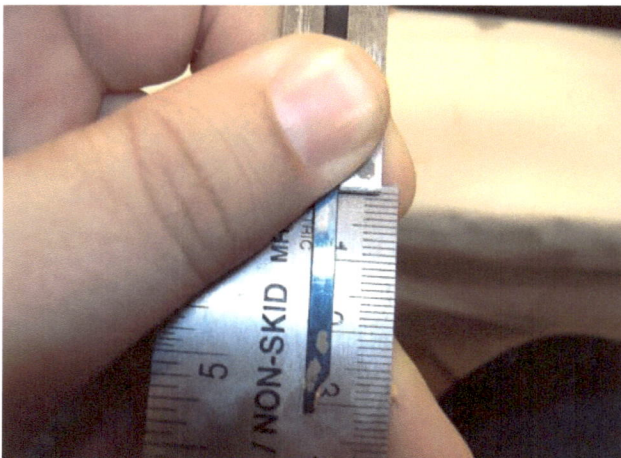

Here is a trick to check the depth. Measure out the depth with the back of the calipers. You will get a spine that sticks out the length you need.

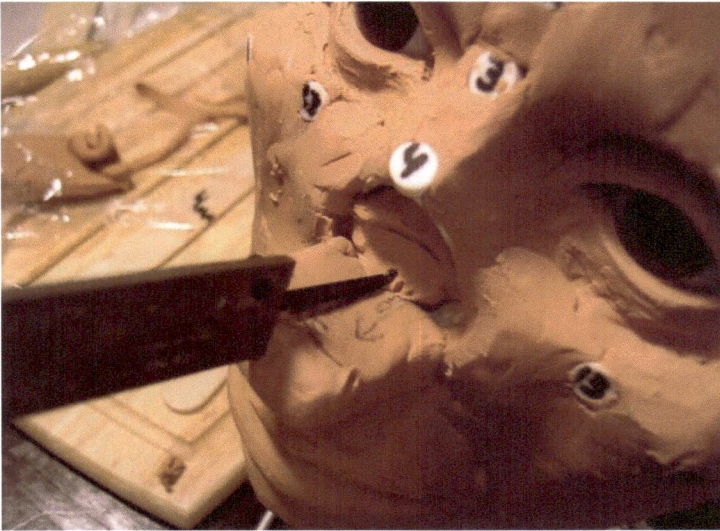

Now check the depth of the clay. If it's off, now is the time to fix it.

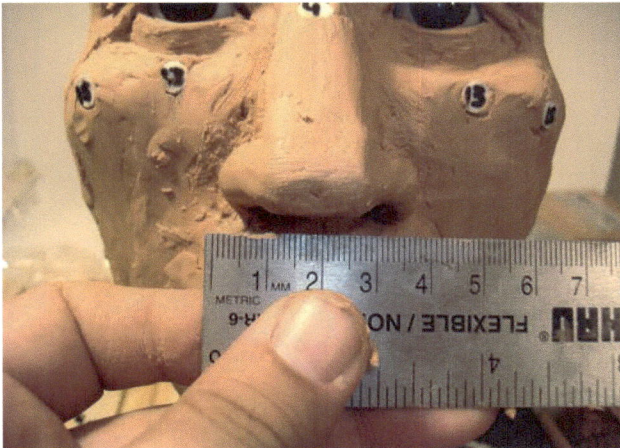

Step 36
Fill in the cavity and the area between the nose and eyes. Do a final measurement check of the width and depth of the nose.

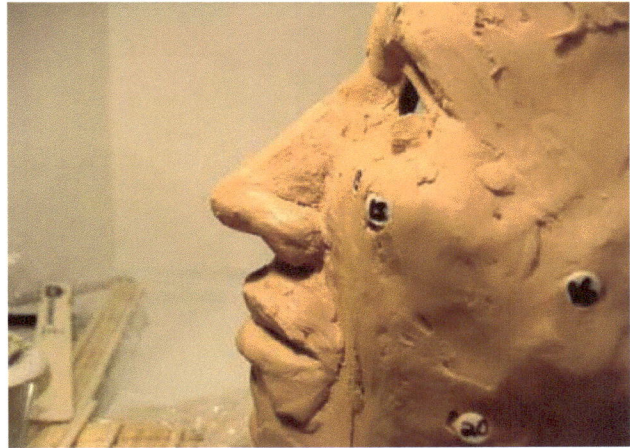

Notice that the nostrils tilt back. This is a subtle feature to look for to achieve a realistic effect.

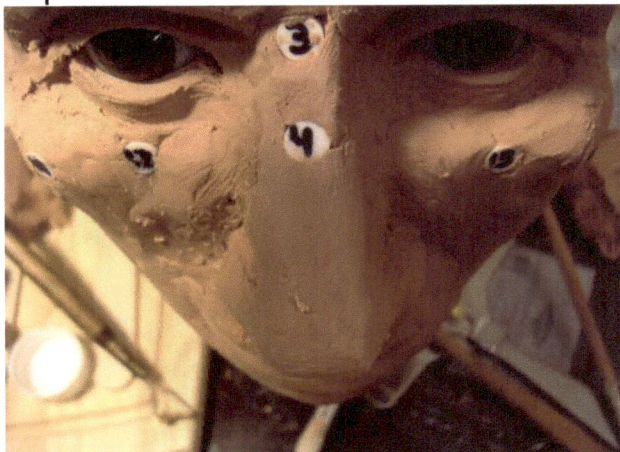

Here is an overview of what we've done so far, including the shapes we used. Use these diagrams to evaluate your work.

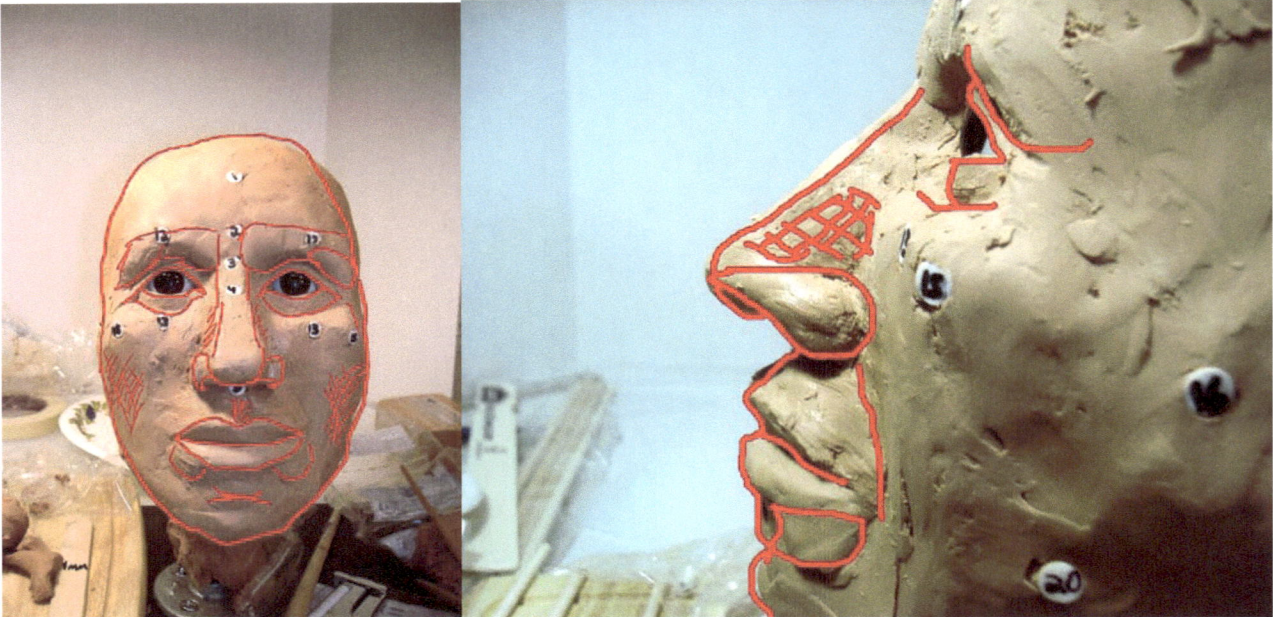

NOW PUT THE PROJECT IN THE FRIDGE!

PART FOURTEEN: FACIAL MUSCLES

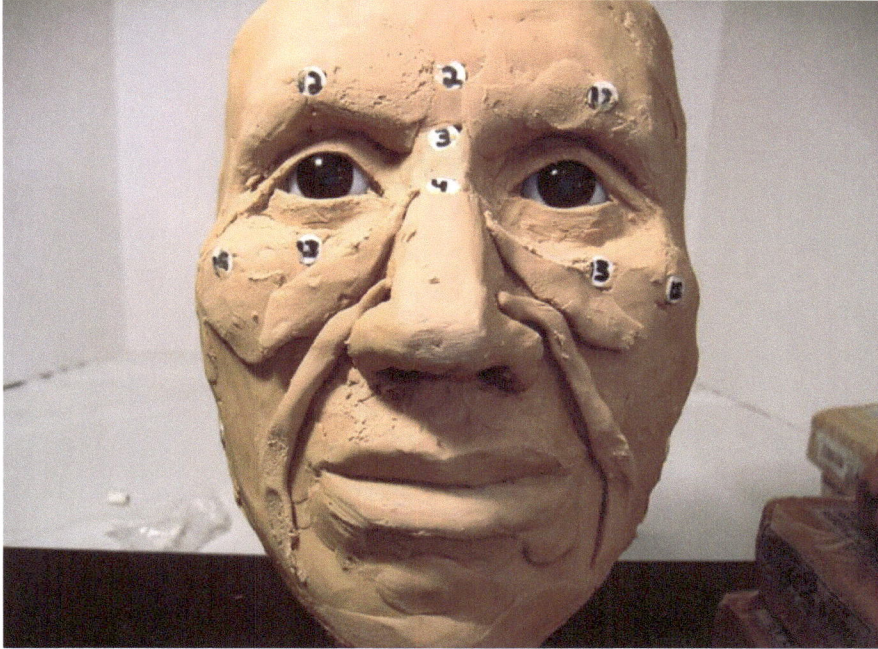

Step 37
Add the facial muscles. Add the muscles that flow off the nose and the folds that are revealed in the nostrils.Try a roll of clay about 5mm thick to start. You may have to adjust the size to proportion.

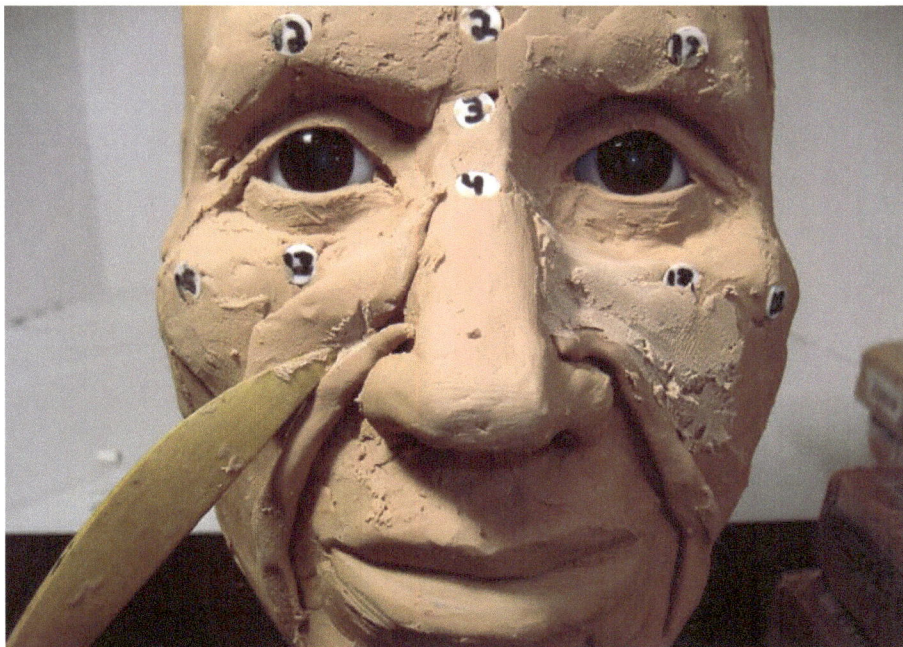

Use a wooden tool to blend them in, BUT NOT WITH YOUR FINGERS! Make sure that the nostril folds are indeed folds and not a ridge. The key is to lay down a snake of clay from the top of the nostrils down to the corner of the mouth, then add bits of clay to the outer edge and blend it in to the cheek area.

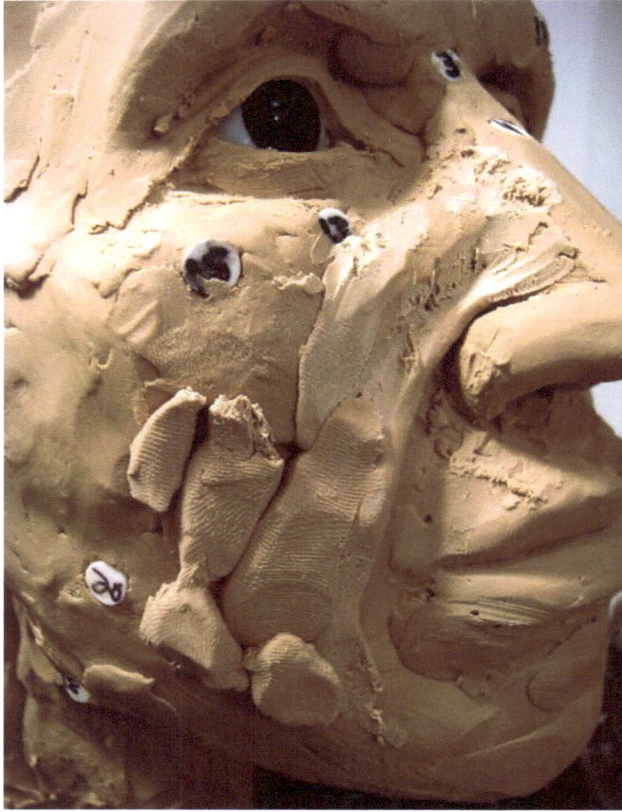

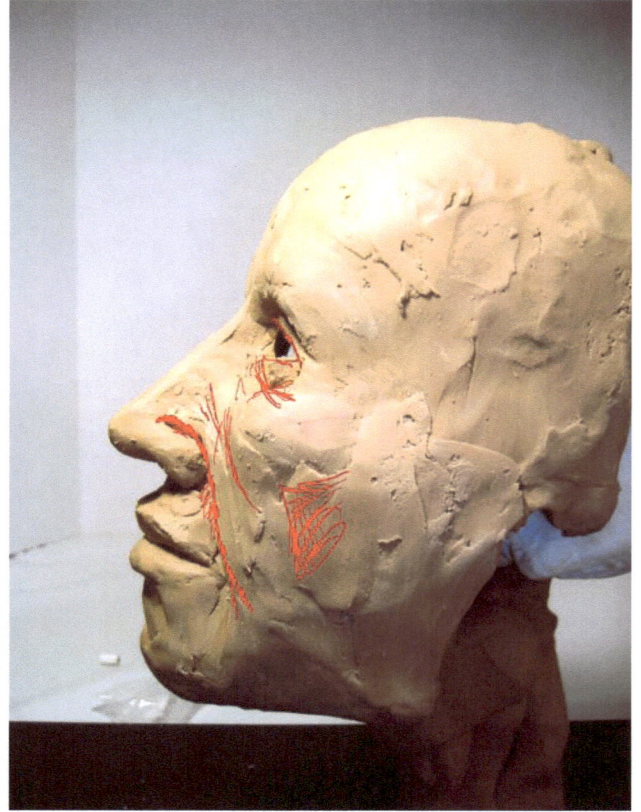

When doing the cheeks and nasal folds, be careful not to create a ridge. Look for references in magazines or anatomy books. Use your mirror as this can be a tough area. Try to mimic what you see on real people. Or, feel your face for the placement of the bones while looking in the mirror.

Make sure the folds off the nostrils are folds, not a ridge. The key is to lay down a snake of clay from the nostrils down to the corner of the mouth then add bits of clay to the outside edge of it and blend it in to the cheek area. I have highlighted the shapes.

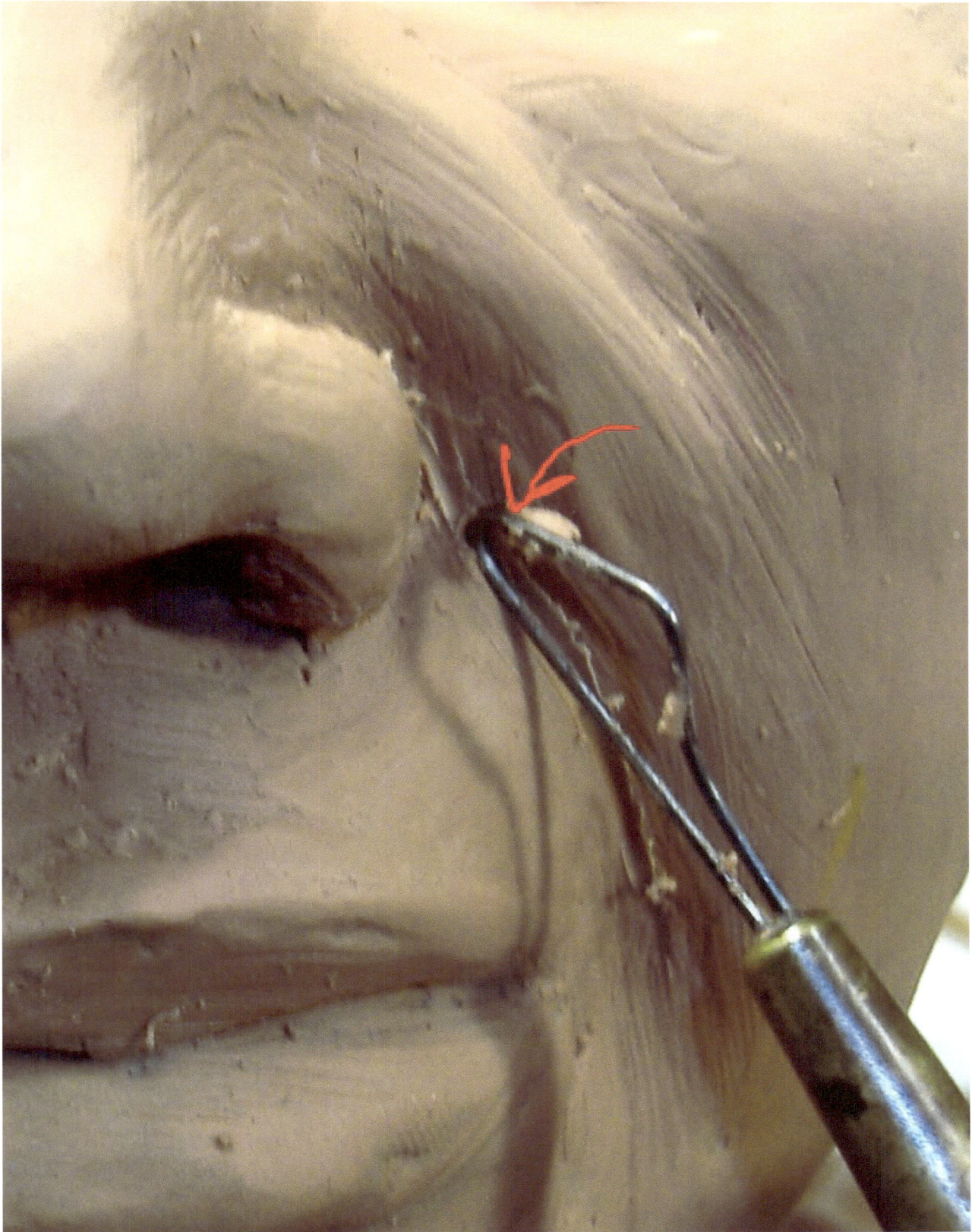

Angle the tool just like when you did the eyelids. This is the best way to sculpt the nasal folds.

To avoid aging the person beyond his or her years, create subtle folds by going across the grain of the fold or wrinkle. Use the widest part of the tool to do this. This will break down the clay. You never want people to say "Look at those wrinkles!" even if it is a positive comment. You want them to say "Look at that person!" or sculpture. Don't allow one feature to dominate the others. The sculpture or head should be seen as a whole.

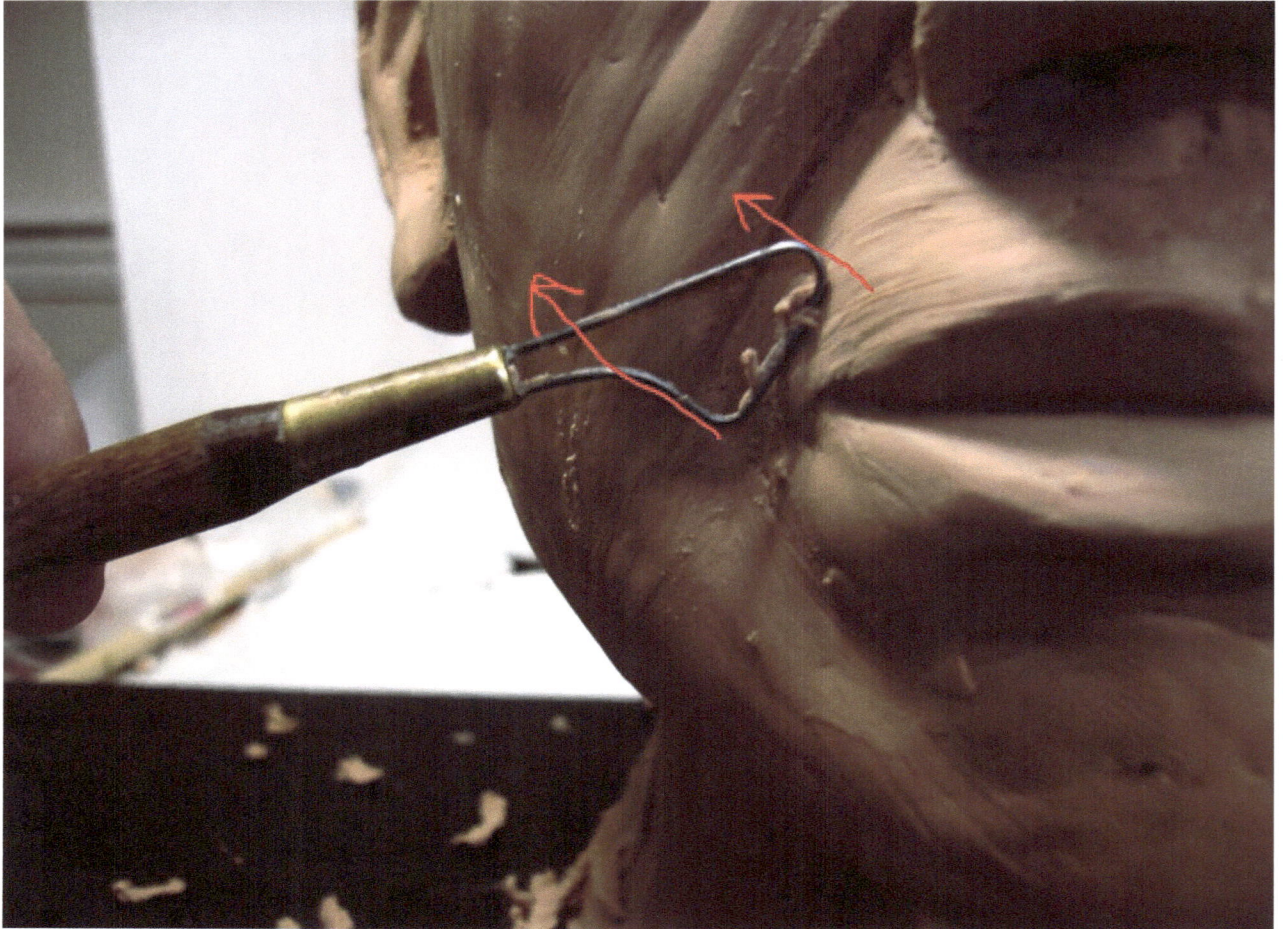

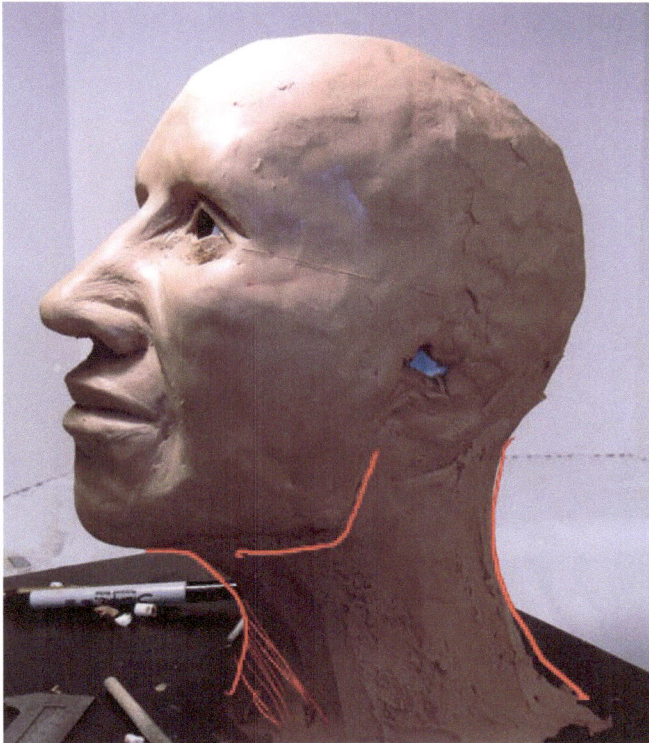

Step 38
Add the neck. Make sure it angles.

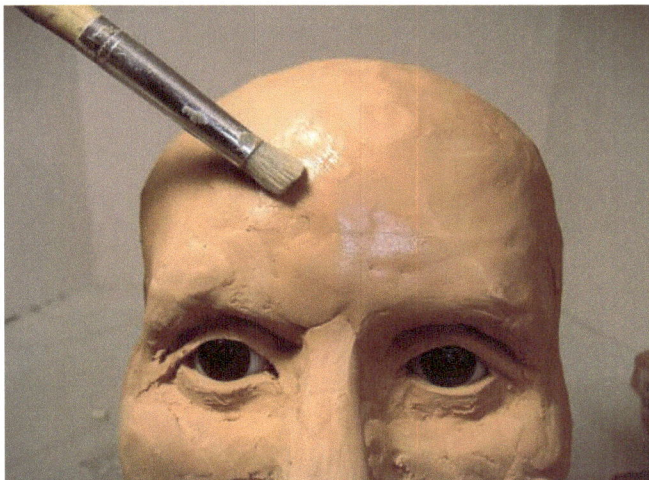

Step 39
Smooth out everything with a stencil brush and alcohol.

PART FIFTEEN: THE EARS

The ears can be the most difficult to make and match up, but they make the head look real. Again, use as much reference as possible. Look from the front, behind, and from above to make sure they are even.

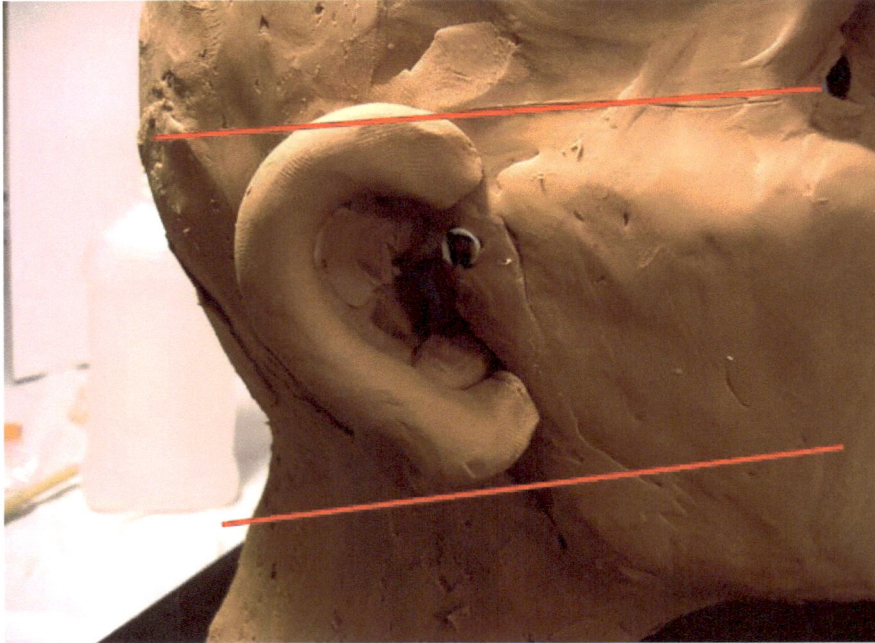

Step 40
To begin the ears, make a large worm of clay. Use this as a guide for placement. Start from about the corner of the eye to the edge of the jaw, with a slight angle backwards.

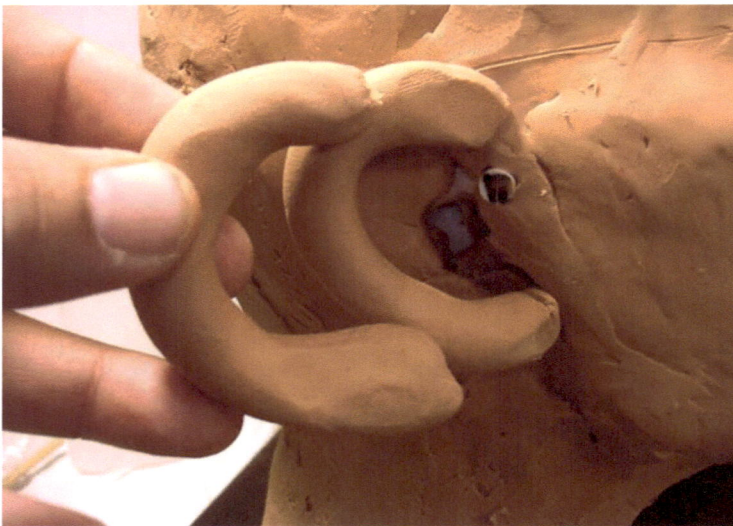

Step 41
Mirror the shape and size for the other side. Do this now, because it will make matching them up easier. Then sculpt them out. Don't rush.

Step 42

Smooth with alcohol and a small brush. Here is the mirrored image of the ear. Don't expect them both to be identical. That's okay. It's also fine to have one ear a little higher or lower. Use references for doing the ears because they are difficult. It requires a bit of practice. Carve the shapes in. Don't be afraid to build up and carve down. But understand, you WILL need to create the ears.

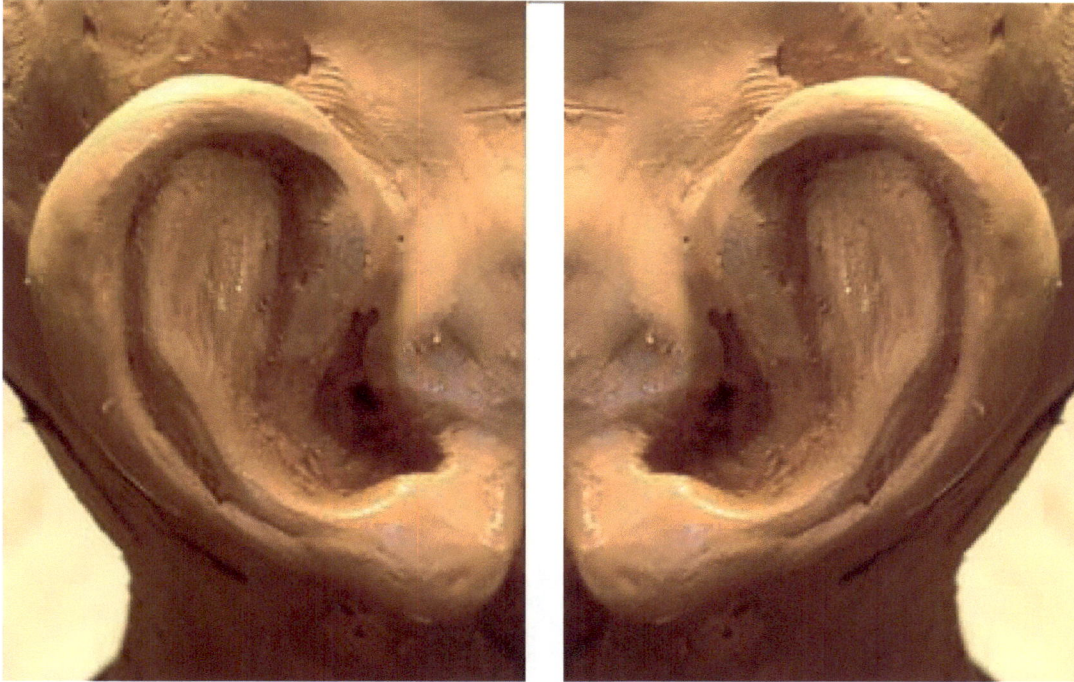

This is roughly what your head should look like at this time. Remember, it won't look identical to mine, however it should look very similar. Finish the project before you decide to completely redo the head. At the very least, this exercise will give you more practice.

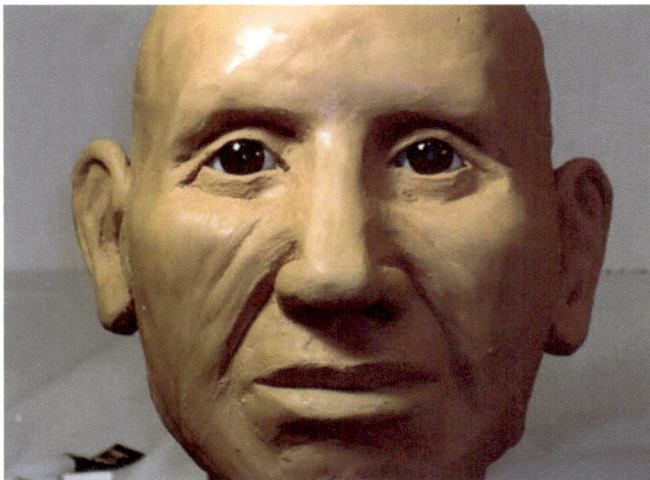

Now look at the head. In my demonstration, the ear on the right is little low, so I will have to fix that. Look at the nasal folds. Again, they should be folds, not ridges. I will study the eyes and adjust them when necessary. Check the nostrils. Recheck your lip, nose sizes, and measurements. It's better to redo all of this work if it means helping to identify a person's remains. Now refrigerate the head overnight. Remember not to compensate for defects in the skull.

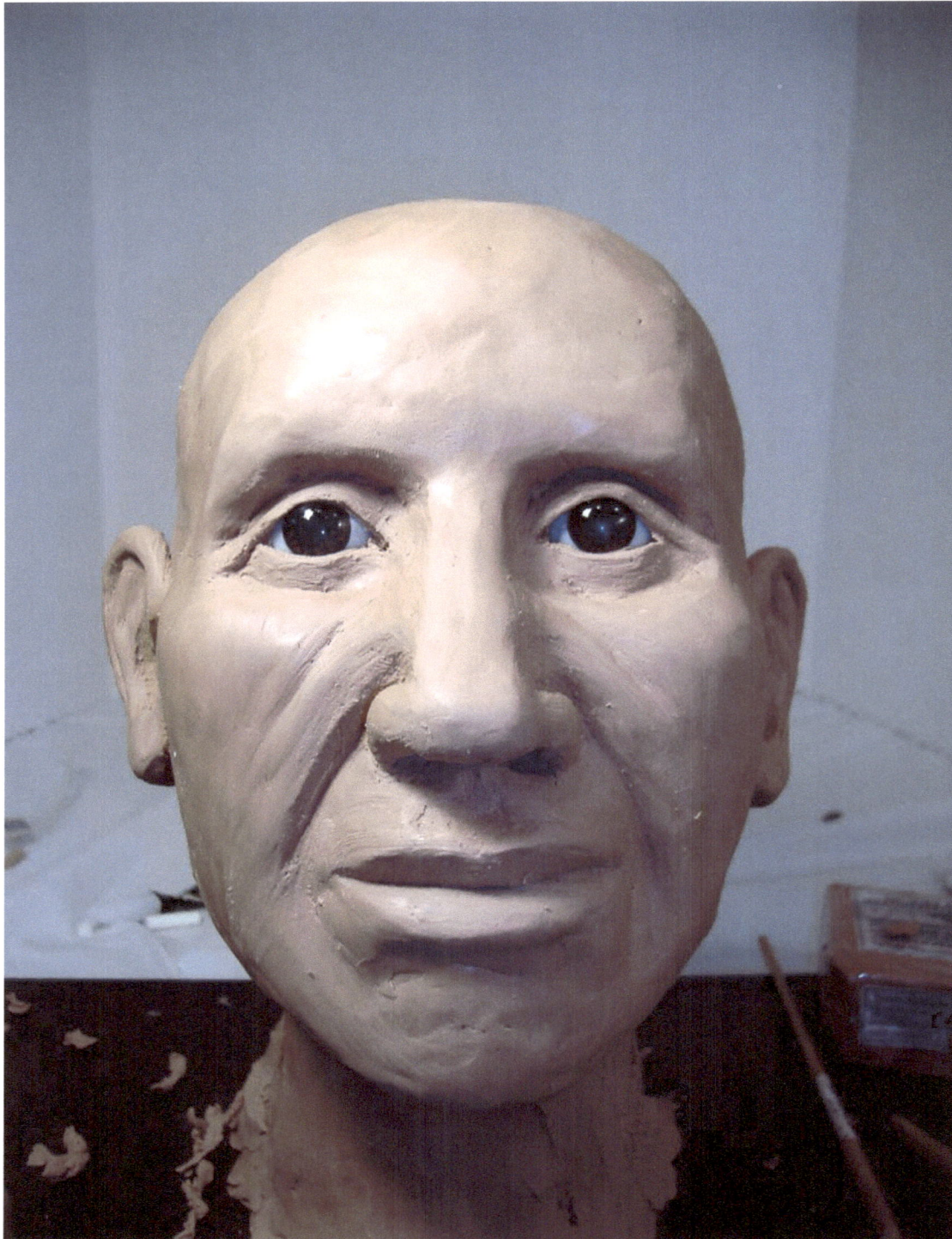

Below, if you look closely at this person's skull, notice they have a curve to the top of the nasal area. It could be an old broken nose, or a crooked nose or even just damage to the skull. You do not try to fix anything that you think is wrong, you just follow the skull. Let an anthropologist determine if there is a problem. As a sculptor you are not qualified to make that sort of judgment.

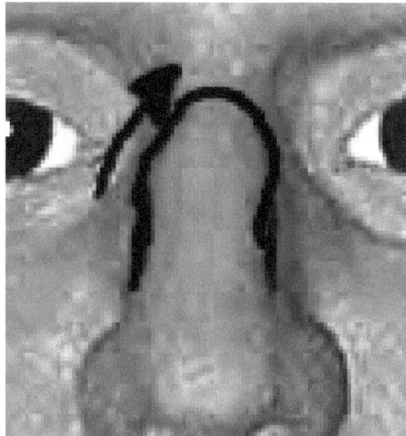

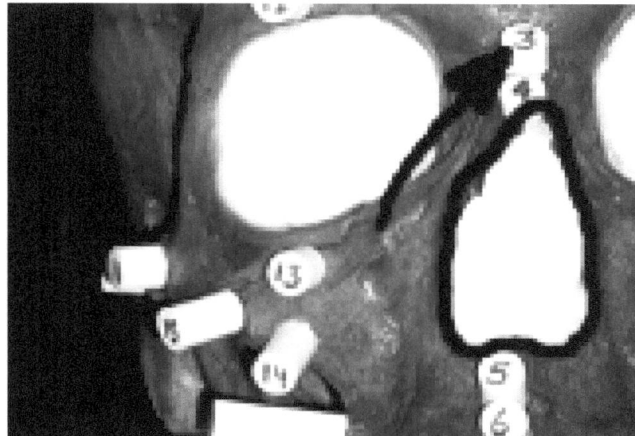

I once created sculpture on a practice skull and thought I had made a mistake because the mouth curved down on one side. Then, when I saw the photo of the real woman, it appeared as if she had a stroke or a muscle disease and as a result, her bone grew into the shape caused by the mystery illness, as an artist I can only follow the bone. An anthropologist may have seen the skull and knew that there was something about the persons health or features, I could only follow the markers. The point is, you just follow the skull, you are not the anthropologist, so let them decide why the skull is a certain way, but do talk to them. When working with a skull sometimes they are damaged, I may have to fill in the tooth area by estimating. In the beginning, I would stay away from major skull reconstructions until you have gained extensive experience. Overall, follow what the skull tells you when in doubt.

PART SIXTEEN: HAIR

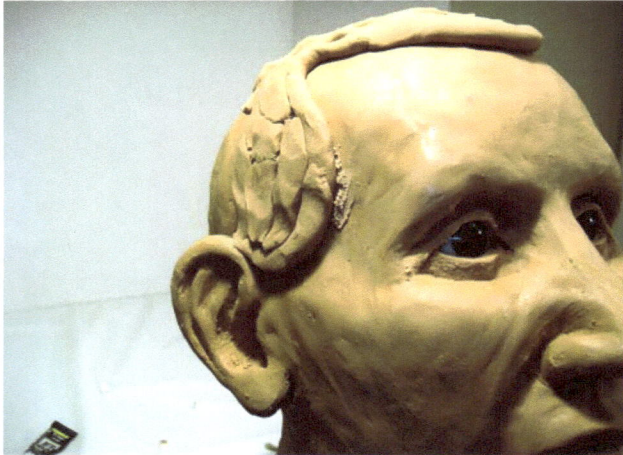

Step 43
Use snakes of clay to block out the hair line. Keep the hair simple; it's just to help complete the head, not to overpower it. You may also use a wig. I personally don't like wigs, but sculpting hair is not everyone's favorite task.

Use a wooden tool to put lines in the clay in the direction that hair would fall. Then brush with alcohol to smooth. I will sometimes use a finer tool with the hairline.

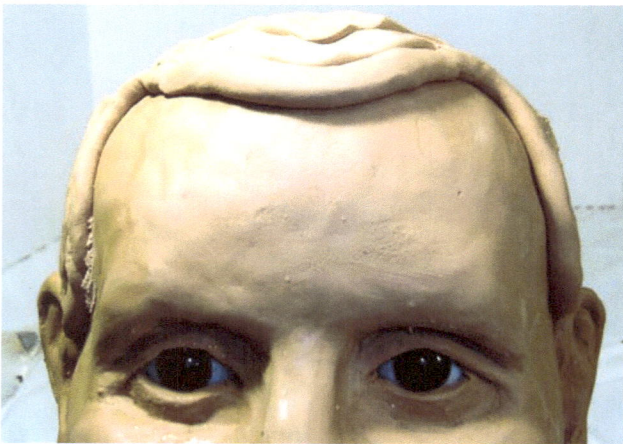

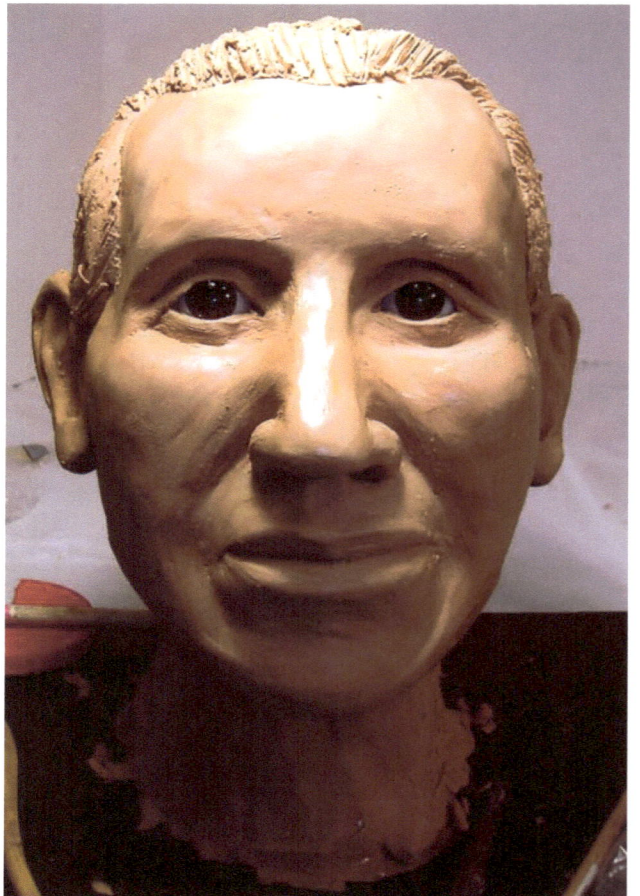

PART SEVENTEEN: TEXTURE AND DETAIL

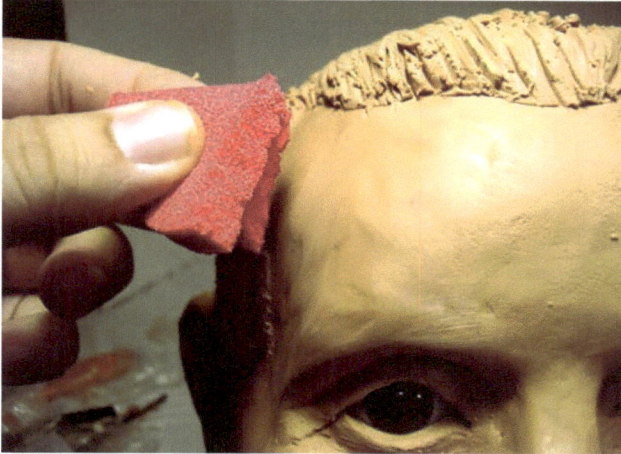

Step 44
First, use a brush and solvent to smooth everything. Then rip a red sponge in half and fold like this to stamp on skin texture. This method is useful for photographing these types of sculptures, but not fine enough for wax figures or fine artwork.

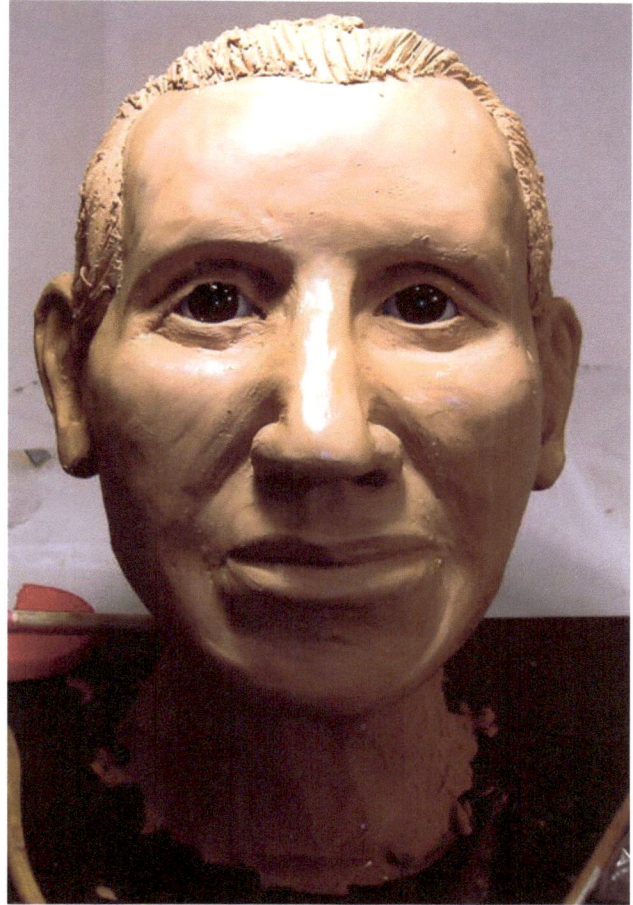

Notice the texture. It may be necessary to press firmly, but be careful not to mash the form of your sculpture.

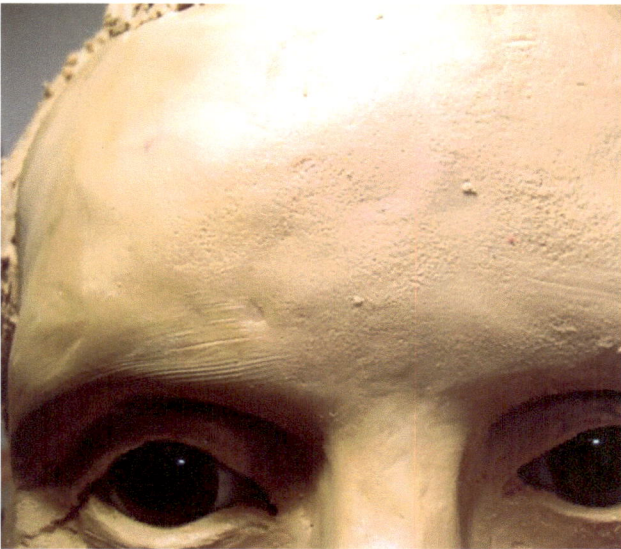

Step 45
Give the sculpture the once over, twice for defects, bumps, uneven nostrils, eyelids and so on. Take your time. Fix what needs to be fixed.

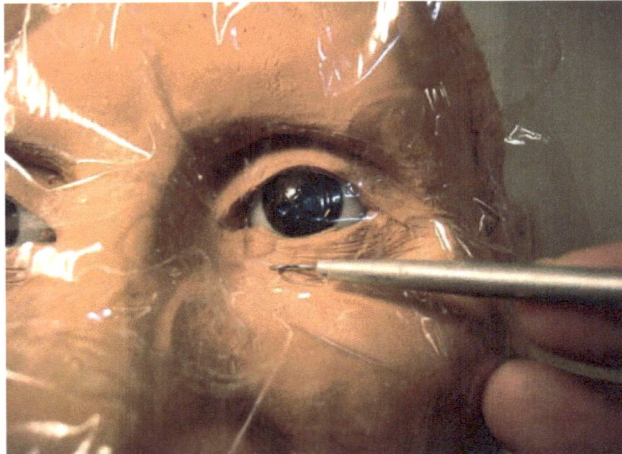

Step 46
Here is a well-kept secret in forensics sculpting: lay plastic wrap over your sculpture, then use the thin end of a tool to create natural wrinkles. What you don't want is obvious grooves cut into the clay.

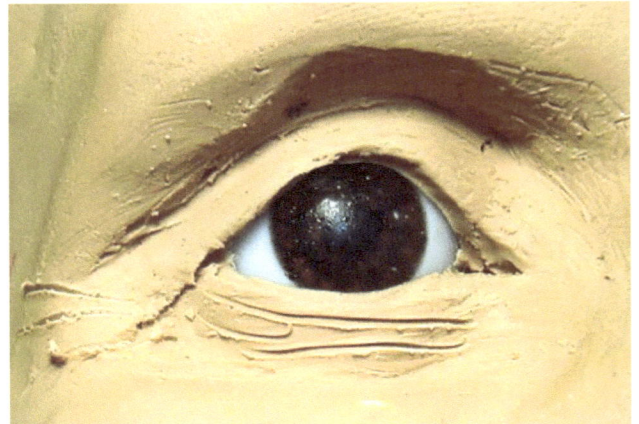

Here are the final eye wrinkles achieved with this method. DON'T OVERDO IT WITH THE EYE WRINKLES unless they are old. Don't use this trick to add character lines that are not there. Creating subtle detail is the objective.

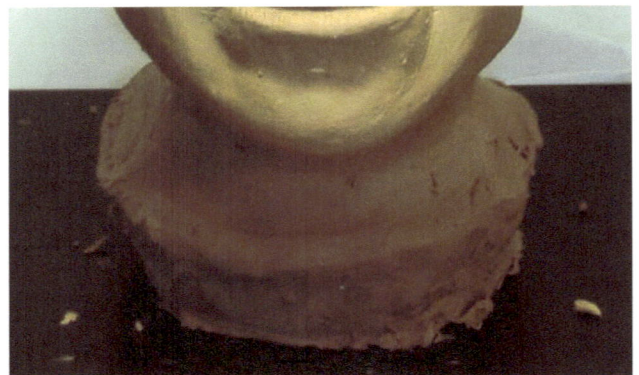

BAD WRINKLES! These look cut "into" the clay, not soft and natural. Fix this problem with a small soft brush and alcohol.

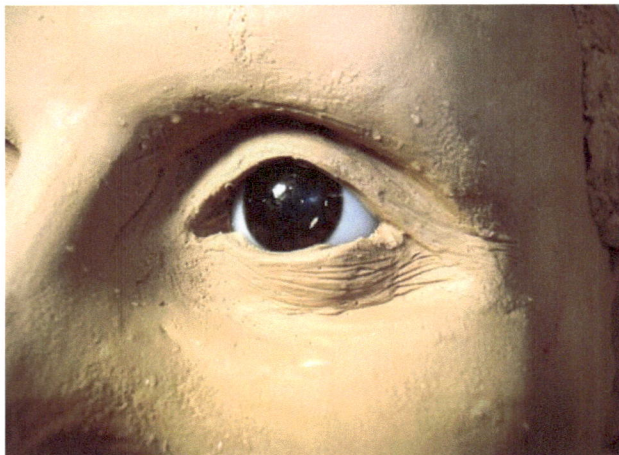

Step 47
Sculpt the base and finish off the neck. Detail the neck by adding an adams apple for males if desired, although not too big. I prefer the sculpted base route. It looks more impressive to me, yet not so "fancy" that it takes away from the sculpture itself.

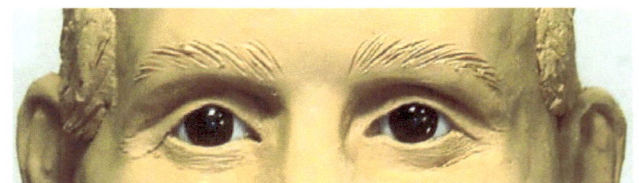

Step 48
Add eyebrows. I cut these in with a directional method.

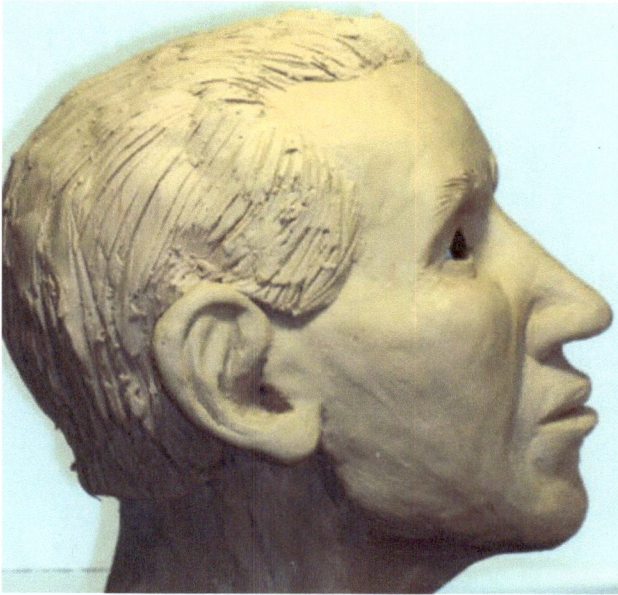

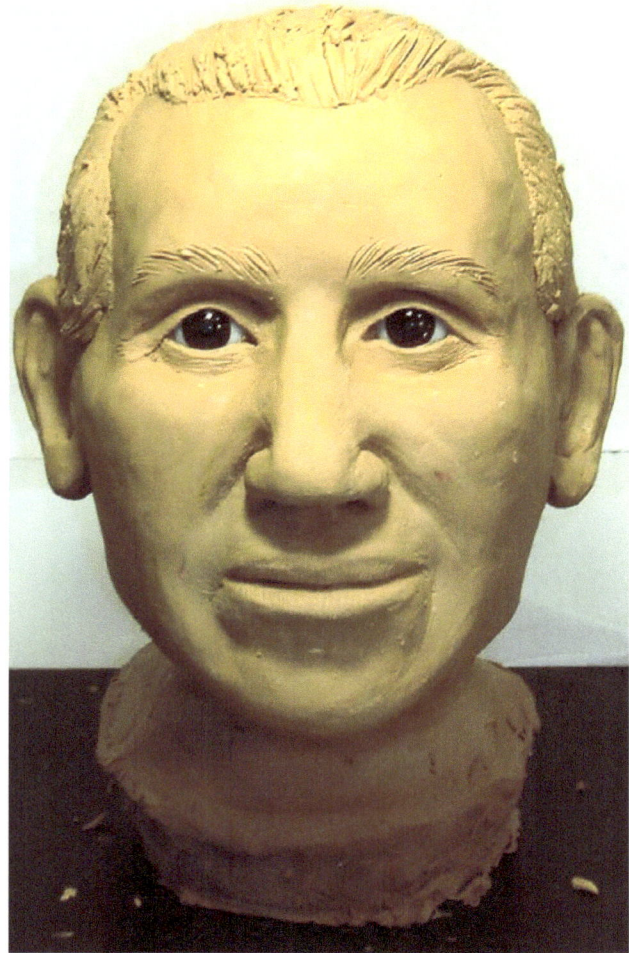

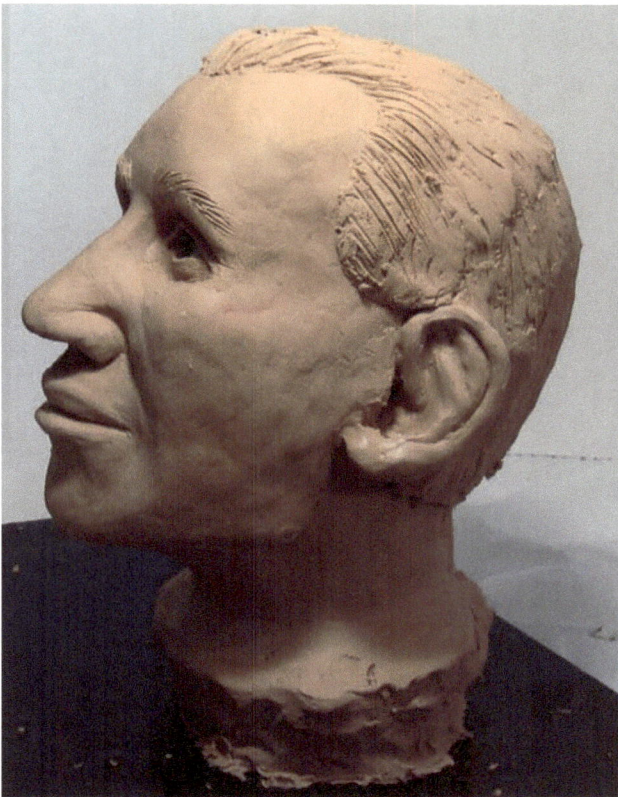

STEP 49

TAKE LOTS OF PHOTOS! The best way to improve you skills is to look at your past work. I prefer black and white finished photography over color because I feel it conveys more realism, there are no colors to confuse or throw off the media. I had an experience where a reporter thought the color of the clay was actually supposed to be the victim's actual skin color.

THE FINAL SCULPTURE

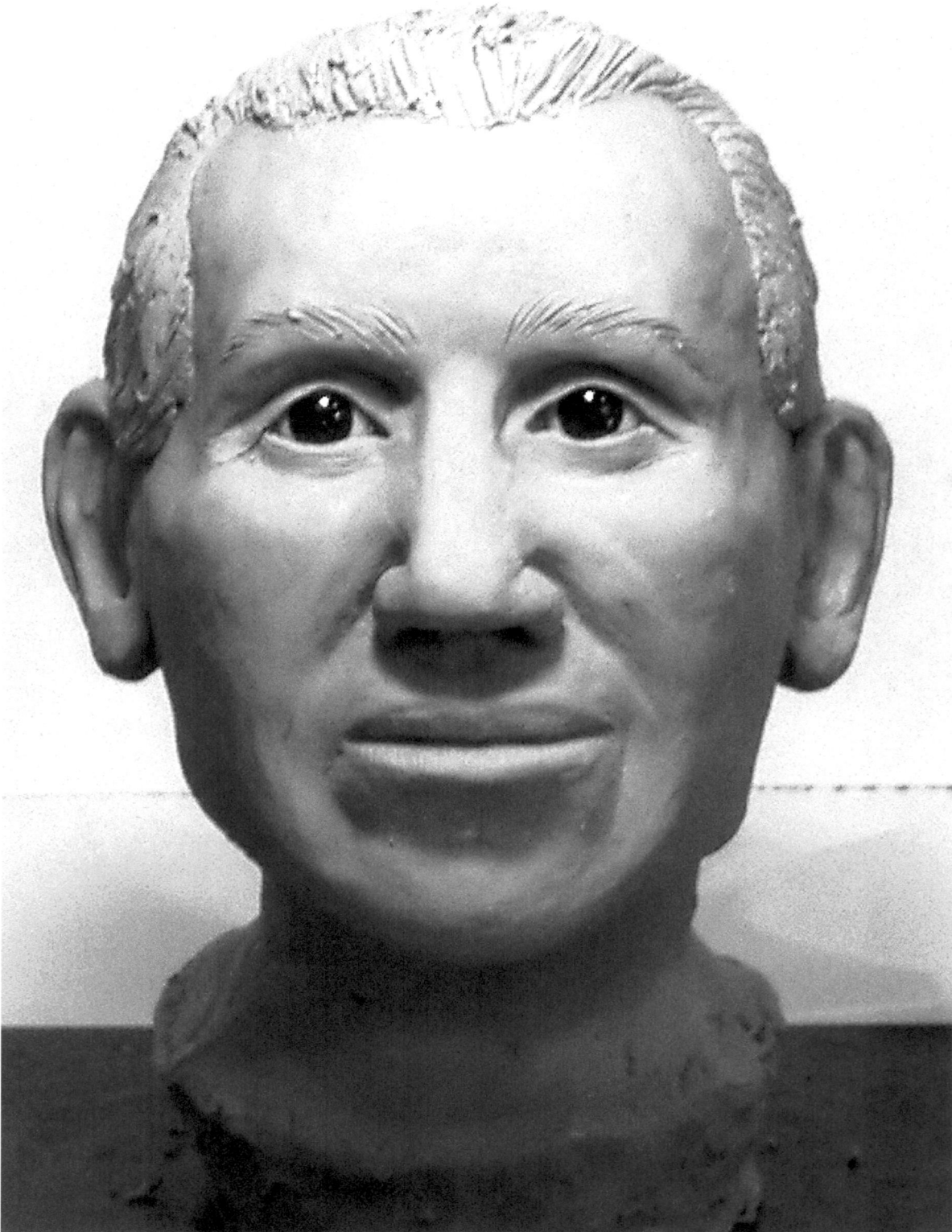

ABOUT THE AUTHOR

Seth Wolfson has been a professional artist and sculptor since 1988. He has been a forensic sculptor for the Bensalem, Pennsylvania Police Department, The Doe Network, and Project EDAN. His figures

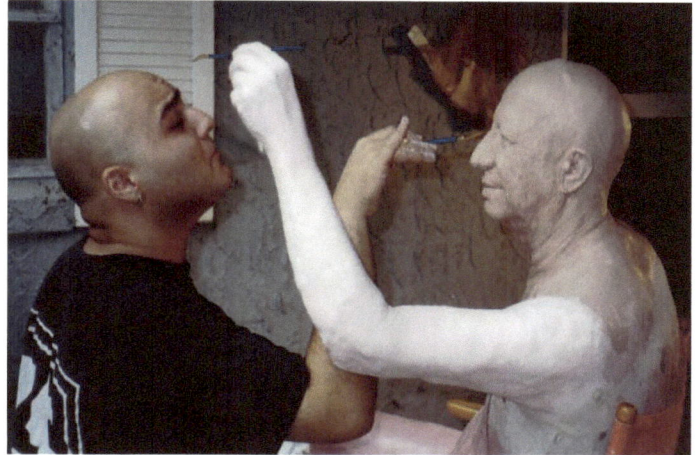

and sculptures can be seen in museums around the world, such as Ripley's Believe It or Not! His work can even be seen at such places as the Portland International Airport in Oregon. He has taught privately and at several large schools such as the Art Institute of Philadelphia since 1994 in the fields of sculpting, mold-making, and make-up FX.

Wolfson has created and worked on life-like animatronic figures for companies such as Universal Studios, and his work can be seen on film and TV, including previously-aired spots/features on the *SciFi Channel* and *Nickelodeon*. He has provided his expertise to commercials, major events, restaurants, production companies, and amusement parks including Nintendo, Disney World's Pleasure Island, Six Flags, and Haxan Films' popular freakylinks.com website.

Wolfson is currently a sculptor for Alatheia Prosthetics, the leading medical prosthetics firm in the country known for making some of the most realistic medical prosthetics in the world.

More of Wolfson's work can be seen at www.realsculpt.com and www.forensicsculpting.com. Any questions regarding this book or booking Wolfson for a seminar, speaking engagement, or media event, please contact him directly through his forensic sculpting website.

Examples of non-forensic realistic figures and movie make-ups (©Seth Wolfson)

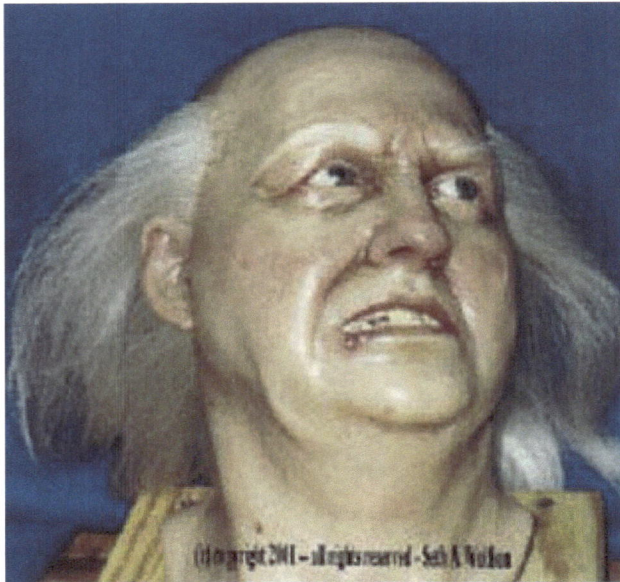
Wax figure

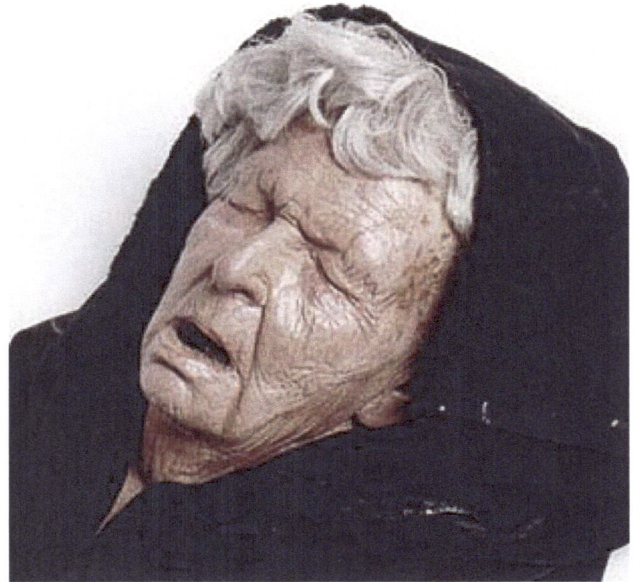
Plaster head painted for a theatrical production

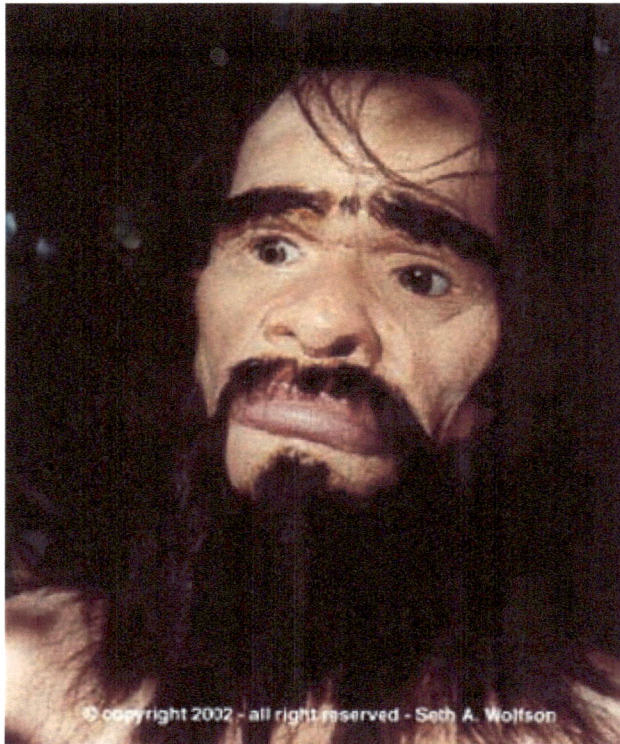
Plastic figure of caveman

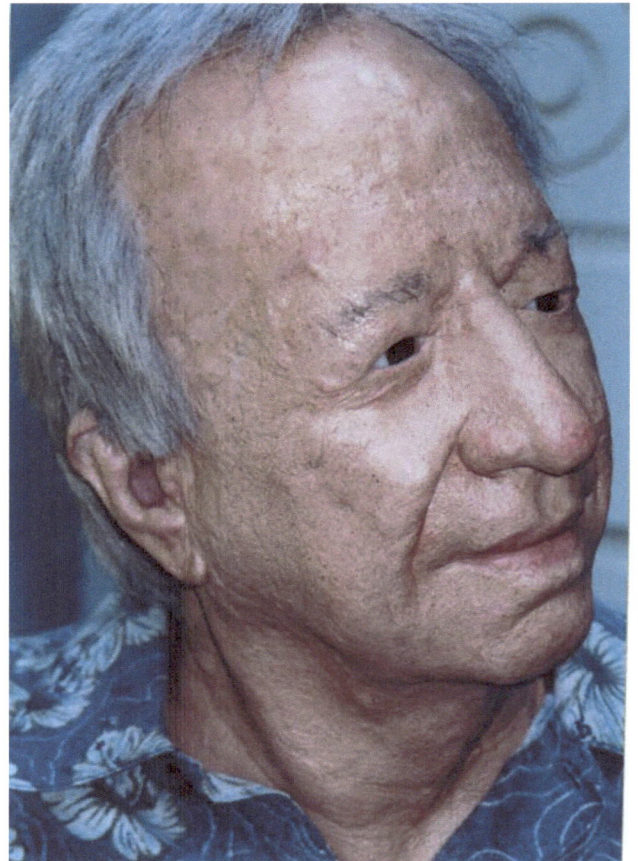
Plastic figure for Portland International Airport

Painted plaster head

"Stretchy face" personal project - foam latex and airbrush

Prop forensic sculpture for a commercial for Iris Johansen's book "Blind Alley"

Personal project of alien prosthetic

BIBLIOGRAPHY

Karen T. Taylor, ed. <u>Forensic Art and Illustration.</u> Boca Raton, Florida: CRC Press, 2001.

Rhine, Dr. Stan. "Re: Permission to use depth charts." E-mail to the author. 21 May 2005.

www.ingramcontent.com/pod-product-compliance
Lightning Source LLC
Chambersburg PA
CBHW041950220326
41599CB00004BA/210

9 781257 503025